W9-CPE-840

Bette Midler

Bette Midler

ACE COLLINS

ST. MARTIN'S PRESS
NEW YORK

Library of Congress Cataloging-in-Publication Data

Collins, Ace.
Bette Midler / Ace Collins.
p. cm.
"A Thomas Dunne Book."
ISBN 0-312-02869-5
1. Midler, Bette. 2. Singers—United States—Biography.
3. Motion pictures actors and actresses—United States—Biography.
I. Title.
ML420.M43C6 1989
784.5'0092'4—dc19
[B] 89-4094
CIP
MN

First U. S. Edition

10 9 8 7 6 5 4 3 2 1

To Beth,
whose life has already been a marvelous profile
in courage and faith

Bette Midler

Introduction

BETTE MIDLER DEFIES DESCRIPTION!

Only a few individuals can so cleverly hide their real persona behind so many different masks and characters, but she is one of those few. So much of her life has been subject to question—even her birthdate—but the one thing that cannot be questioned is her enormous talent. Her uniqueness, her one-of-a-kind personality and look, that special kind of trashy style have all made her not only a superb performer, but a fascinating person as well.

Who is Bette Midler? She has been shaped by experience, tragedy, failure, and success. Yet to begin to understand the real Bette, you must look at her beginnings . . . as well as a climb to the top that was often far from divine.

Bette Midler has now reached a period that is often referred to as middle-aged. She seems to have a firm grasp on her life, her future, and her identity. She could have suffered the same fate as Janis Joplin (a woman who indirectly gave Bette her first shot at movie stardom), Jimi Hendrix, Marilyn Monroe, or even Elvis—experiencing the emptiness of a life without love and satisfaction, a lonely but demanding existence marked by the fear that failure would come at any moment, and that there would no longer be enough talent left to go on. Bette found herself in this trap. Yet not only did she survive, but she has discovered a fullness of life that is reserved for the truly successful.

Bette Midler's road to personal discovery is almost as interesting as her road to fame and fortune. For as much as any person she is a woman shaped by her roots, her name, and her environment. She has molded herself into one of the world's most unlikely superstars, and her story is like a fantasy fairy tale, an unpredictable ride on a show business roller coaster. In the words of another Bette, "It is going to be a bumpy ride."

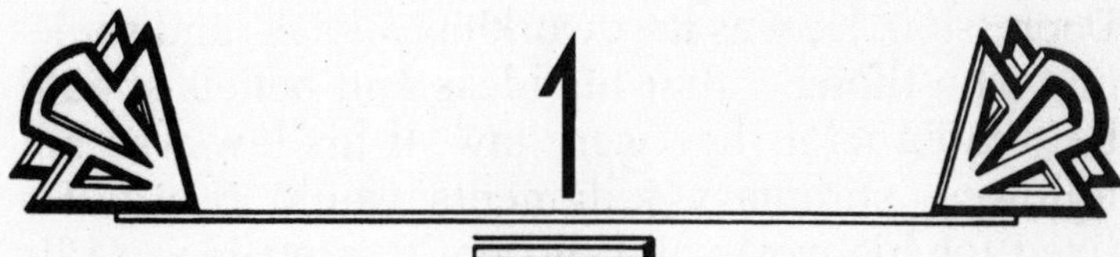

1

Many sources incorrectly list Patterson, New Jersey as Bette Midler's birthplace. While it is true that her roots go back to this East Coast city, the future Divine Miss M was born in paradise—or at least what most of us would view as paradise—Honolulu, Hawaii on December 1, 1944. She wasn't born into great wealth or even middle-class society. Like so many entertainers, she was brought into a world that provided just the few material things necessary for survival. There were no luxuries.

Her father, Fred, a Jewish, New Jersey-born housepainter, had moved his family to the islands in the late thirties. He had said when he left his hometown that he wanted to find "heaven on earth," but most relatives and friends agreed that his definition of that imaginary place would be the farthest English-speaking location from his overbearing mother. Yet as he moved his family to this paradise looking for peace, he found just the opposite. Within a few months of moving, the Midlers would be directly in the middle of a world war.

Fred Midler was not that much different from millions of other men who'd been shaped by the Depression. He was hardworking, a loner, and someone who thought that his ideas and beliefs should be treated as if they were law. If his law was not followed, summary judgments would result. He lived for his work, and did not waste time in idle dreaming. Surviving spelled success, and little else was necessary.

For this painter, work was not easy to find. The Hawaii of the time was not an area filled with many residential or commercial buildings. By and large, it was still a small group of islands thought of more as an exotic locale than as a place to move or set up business. Besides, who wanted to live someplace that the Japanese might bomb again? Therefore, as the Midler family grew, the family finances didn't, and life was tough.

While employment opportunities for Fred Midler were far from stable, his wife, a beautiful, delicate woman named Ruth, was like a rock to her husband. She had left her roots and followed him without question to the islands, knowing that she was leaving behind the only friends and family she had ever had. And even more than that, she was journeying to a place where Jews were as hard to find as needles in haystacks.

Once she arrived in the islands, however, Ruth continued to support her husband's decisions, even when she didn't understand them. No matter what, she encouraged him, stood by him, and loved him, and he knew that she would always be there for him. She was a good wife and prided herself on it.

Ruth was much different than Fred, and it was not difficult to wonder what had brought the two of them together. She was a dreamer, someone who loved to get dressed up and go out. She enjoyed movies and plays, and loved to read the classics. She thrived around people, and longed for a lifetime of new experiences. But by marrying Fred, what she really got was a government-subsidized house (more like a shack) in the middle of a large sugarcane field and years of poverty. Still, she made the best of it, never forgetting her dreams—or the movies.

No matter how poor they were, Ruth always scraped together enough loose change to spend a dime down at the local theater. There she saw the likes of Gary Cooper, Humphrey Bogart, and James Cagney. While she loved to watch these giants in action, her real favorites—the screen stars that she identified with most—were the women: Myrna Loy, Jean Harlow, and Claudette Colbert. These stars caught her fancy and imagination, and provided a much-needed escape from the drudgery of poverty.

So, it wasn't that unusual that when Ruth's first daughter was born, she was named after her mother's favorite movie star, Judy Garland. A few years later, her second daughter was named after one of Hollywood's hottest new actresses, Susan Hayward. Then, in late 1944, for her third little girl, Ruth once again turned to Hollywood for inspiration and a name.

She had seen a certain dynamic, fascinating, and fiery actress at the theater on countless occasions. Ruth never said what had impressed her the most about the Warner Bros. star, but it might have been her courage and strength. After all, with the United States in the middle of a bloody war, and with Hawaii having been hit with the full force of the Japanese war machine, Ruth Midler may have felt that a little girl growing up during these times would need both of these attributes. What she probably didn't guess at that time was that her little girl would also receive a great deal of her namesake's brashness, honesty, and independence.

From the first day at the Honolulu hospital where she was born, little Bette was called "Bet" rather than Betty, simply because Ruth Midler had never heard the proper pronunciation of Bette Davis's name. If she had, there is little doubt that the woman we know as the Divine Miss M would have come to us with a first name that had two, rather than one, syllables. As it was, the proud mother thought she was calling her daughter by a great star's name.

During baby Bette's first year, the United States won World War II, and the islands returned to a certain degree of peace. One immediate result was a building boom. Bombed-out homes and military installations were repaired and rebuilt, and with a wider range of American influence in the Pacific region, many installations were enlarged and new ones added. Still, the high cost of living, coupled with the relatively cheap native labor force, left Fred Midler with little more income than he had been receiving before the war. Prosperity may have hit the islands, but it did not hit the Midler household.

Bette and her sisters grew up in a world that was the total opposite of most young Jewish-Americans of the period. Unlike her mainland relatives, grouped together by tradition, religion, and community, the Midlers were alone with their heritage. There simply were no other Jews in and around the small rural town of Aiea. As a matter of fact, there were no other whites in the area. Still, this isolation went largely unnoticed by Bette until she went to first grade.

Ruth Midler was the main reason the family didn't look as poor as they were. She was an excellent seamstress, and could fashion just about anything into new outfits for her kids. No extra fabric was wasted, and everything was either passed down or transformed. When the material ran out, the local Salvation Army store became the family boutique. During these sprees, Ruth and her little girls must have felt like they were shopping at Macy's. They simply made do and chose to ignore their economic situation.

The Midlers had an old metal shower outside their home, and it was always obvious when someone was in the shower and who it was. Neighborhood children would often bang on the shower's walls to hear the long ringing sound the metal would make, or see what wet and naked person would come flying out. Also, stacked all around the home were scores of old lawn mowers and other machines that Fred liked to collect. He always intended to fix them and sell them, but he never did, and the landscaping resembled Early 20th Century Junkyard.

Inside the house things were spartan. Furniture, although well-kept by Ruth, was old and used. Extra material and clothes were stacked everywhere. It would be the late fifties before the family would buy a television or install a telephone. Except for the radio, books offered the only form of escape and entertainment at home.

Soon after the war ended, another baby, this one a boy named David, joined the three Midler girls. They were still too poor to afford the children they had, much less another one. And as an added burden, David was born retarded, which would tend to isolate the family even further.

When the unique-looking (many people called her ugly) little Bette began first grade, all of her classmates were either of Polynesian, Japanese, or Chinese extraction. She was the only reddish-brown-headed, fair-skinned child in her class. Because she was so very different, she became the center of attention. It may have been this difference that formed the roots of her very unique personality.

Yet at school, Bette Midler was terribly alone. She did not fit in with the natives or locals—their food, their customs, their religion, and their home life were far different from hers. And even if they hadn't been different, her appearance would point out the stark contrast between herself and her classmates. But if she wasn't Hawaiian, what was she?

There were no role models for Bette at home either. Fred Midler, perhaps due to his inability to carve his own paradise out of the one surrounding him, was often ill-tempered, and at times made his children uncomfortable in their own small home. He laid down strict rules: His daughters were not to wear makeup, date, or be out any later than ten o'clock. While Bette was too young in 1951 to worry about these things, she still resented the treatment she and her sisters received from her father. Life was harsh enough without a father making it worse.

Many years later, after she had become a superstar, Bette described her childhood as "grim." While the poverty she experienced was certainly a factor in her appraisal, there is little doubt that her father's temper and restrictions also created problems. Fred Midler was in many ways far too similar to his mother. Without even realizing it, he was driving his children away just as his mother had driven him to move to Hawaii.

In addition to her restrictive home life, what probably did as much to shape Bette's future as any early experience was an elementary school talent program. The carrot-topped first-grader decided to enter, and she picked out the Christmas carol "Silent Night" to sing. Her loud voice, as well as her ability to stay on key, earned her first prize. She was thrilled. But she couldn't decide how to break the news to her Jewish mother that she had sung a traditional Christian holiday song to win a contest. Finally, after hours of searching for the best course of action, she simply confessed. Ruth was overjoyed. She cared little about the song or its subject—she was simply proud that one of her daughters was developing a love for performing.

"Silent Night" gave Bette some much-needed confidence, and she immediately decided that other little girls could become nurses and housewives—she was going to be a singer. The one place that Bette loved to show off her skills was in the outdoor metal shower. There, she received her first critical notices. The local children would often come to listen to Bette bathe, hollering for certain favorites and making fun of her renditions of other tunes. Bette's personal favorite, "Lullaby of Broadway," would echo back and forth across the sugarcane fields every day. Ironically, the shower seemed to be the only place the little girl had a great deal of self-confidence. Everywhere else, she seemed very shy, almost withdrawn.

Ruth wanted to encourage her daughter's love of performing, so in order to help her break out of her shell, she would take Bette to movies whenever there was enough money for tickets. There, in the movie showhouses, the little girl was introduced to the fantasy world her mother had loved for so long. Here Bette could pretend to be a Judy Garland or Grace Kelly. Here were stories of entertainers—like Fanny Brice—who were popular, successful, and Jewish. On the screen were people who looked like her, that she could relate to. Here were real role models.

When Bette wasn't at the movies or in school, she was reading. As she grew older, she moved from simple tales to steamy novels of romance about the Deep South. For the young girl, any escape from her out-of-place life was welcome relief. And books offered her a cheap way to pass many hours and live many lives. One book that she didn't outgrow, that continued to influence her and recapture her attention, was *Alice in Wonderland.*

By the time Bette began junior high, she was wearing rather ugly and thick-framed glasses, carrying too much weight, and had a bosom that was large for a grown woman, much less a girl of her age. In the New Jersey of the midfifties there were probably thousands of young ladies who looked the same sort of nerdy way, but in her school, there was only Bette. Going through puberty is hard enough on any young woman, but in this case, it was exceedingly painful because Bette was so different. The kids constantly made fun of her. As she grew older, she also grew more withdrawn, due in no small part to her looks.

Home was still little better than school. Even though Bette was well-endowed, her father wouldn't let her wear a bra, makeup, or hose. She was stuck being a child with a woman's body, and her father's restrictions were as frustrating for her as they'd been for her sisters. If anyone got home after ten, Fred Midler would lock them out of the house. Movies and books still offered Bette a chance to escape to other worlds, but she was becoming less and less satisfied with these temporary fixes.

She dreamed of running away and living a life far from poverty and strict rules.

Just a short walk from her home was a Navy base. And just a short walk from there was Hawaii's biggest red-light district. It was there that young Bette would often run when she didn't want to go home. The teenager didn't really understand just how rough it was for the local prostitutes. All she knew was that these women were free to do what they wanted, to dress and express themselves in whatever manner they chose. Bette loved the prostitutes' wild, bright clothing and bizarre makeup, the way they walked and talked, their jokes, their painted-on beauty. (These women may well have influenced Bette's own stage fashion later on.) This freedom *seemed* to make them happy. She didn't realize at the time it was acting at its best.

Trying to bring fun to Bette's life, Ruth saved her money and took her daughter to the city to see the musical *Carousel.* It was Bette's visit to the theater, with its color, artistry, music, and costumes that brought a whole new dimension to her life. Ruth could tell that even more than the movies, this production had captured her daughter's imagination. Bette's desire to perform was stronger now than it had been when she was a child singing in the shower.

Once in high school, though still the only white girl in her class, Bette became more and more involved in drama. She took classes, tried out for parts, and even formed a trio with two other girls, called The Pieredine Three. The music they performed was mostly folk, and no one heralded them as Hawaii's answer to the Shirelles, but it did do two things for Bette. First, it gave her some time away from home. Second, it provided her with an opportunity to sing and perform, giving her a bit of self-confidence and stage experience.

By her junior year, though, Bette felt more like a nerd than a class favorite. Still more at home with her books, her songs, and her movies than she was communicating with other people, she didn't have enough self-esteem to take charge and cut loose. Then, one of her friends, an outgoing, fun-loving girl named Beth Eillen Childers, began to encourage her to "get wild." Little by little, through this goading, Bette began to try to fit in with her classmates by being funny, and then loud. Taking Beth's lead, she had fun. For the first time, she acted like a teenage girl, blossoming into a rock'n'roller, a teenybopper, a bandstander, and all the other things that had long been lurking in the nightmares of Fred Midler.

She also rebelled against her father's rules, beginning to dress more like a woman than a girl, and she began to demand that people notice her. She told jokes and even intentionally made a fool of herself in order to gain attention. This was a far cry from the Bette who had entered high school hoping that no one would notice that she existed.

Bette's classmates quickly decided that she was really funny, so Bette always went that extra mile to be even funnier. She would look goofy, dress goofy, or act goofy—and few people took her seriously, which she capitalized on. Tossing off her inhibitions completely, she auditioned for and won the lead in her junior class play. On opening night, Ruth even brought her roses to the footlights, and Bette played the role of the star to the hilt. It was a role she knew she would grow to love.

By the time she was a senior, Bette was so popular and so loud that she was voted one of the school favorites. She was also elected class president and won a state speech contest by reciting a scene from *The Glass Menagerie.* But there was more to her than what her classmates saw. Unlike the other kids, she had plans for an escape.

Bette had by then decided that she wanted out of Hawaii. She wanted to be somewhere that she fit in, and she picked New York as *her* paradise. She knew that her strength was acting, and she also knew—if she played her cards right—that her talent might get her there. But it was going to take something more than a high school play to get her what she wanted. She applied herself to her books and managed to graduate as class valedictorian, an accomplishment that even made her father proud. This guaranteed her a ticket to the University of Hawaii, and a move out of her parents' home. Now she was free to be herself.

The university was supposed to be the answer to all of Bette's teenage problems. But college didn't really challenge Bette or give her much of a chance to be herself. Nor would it immediately give her the performing experience she needed; she just didn't have the right look for the parts. She was confused about her future, and in 1963, many others were confused about theirs, too. A President had just been killed. For nineteen-year-old Bette, a girl who had just recently discovered how to have fun, it was a time when she wasn't ready to worry about the world or its problems. She wanted to laugh. And for a while she did, until a phone call informed her that her best friend, Beth, had died in a car crash. Suddenly the world became a very serious place. It was time for Bette to grow up.

Quitting school, the five-foot, one-inch redhead began to search the main island for work. After a short stint as a secretary at a radio station, she then worked at odd jobs before ending up as the person who separated the center slices in a pineapple factory. In the two short years since she had escaped her home in a sugarcane field, this talented, bright, energetic young woman had dropped out of college and become a common laborer. She seemed to be an eternity away from her dreams of escaping by becoming a star. And even more seriously, she was setting herself up to fall back into the same hole of poverty that she had wanted so badly to leave behind her.

For Bette Midler, the funny-looking Jewish girl who had once seemed so out of place in both her home and her school, it must have been scary to look around at the people in the plant and realize that the heritage that had separated her as a youth was still making her different. She didn't fit in. And the harder she looked, the more difficult an escape appeared.

The way out of Hawaii, however—the one that Bette so desperately wanted—lay just ahead. And even though she couldn't have foreseen it, much less dreamed it, her ticket to the mainland would have a big *Hawaii* stamped right in the middle of it. But that was several months and a few thousand pineapples in her future.

BETTE WAS WORKING IN THE FRUIT-CANNING FACTORY in 1965 when the filming schedule for the movie *Hawaii* was announced. *Hawaii,* an adaptation of James Michener's epic novel, was planned as a film to celebrate the nation's newest state and paint vivid pictures of this paradise and its history.

The starring and supporting roles were pinned down by the time the crew arrived on location to start filming. The era's hottest female lead, Julie Andrews, who'd dazzled in *Mary Poppins, The Americanization of Emily,* and *The Sound of Music,* would star. Opposite her was Max von Sydow, probably best known for his portrayal of Christ in *The Greatest Story Ever Told.*

Others in the cast would include such future heavyweights as Gene Hackman, Carroll O'Connor, and Richard Harris, as well as a well-known Indian actor, Torin Thatcher. A young director,

George Roy Hill, was chosen as the director. He was coming off a highly regarded hit, *The World of Henry Orient* (and his best work would come later with *Slaughterhouse Five, Butch Cassidy and the Sundance Kid,* and *The Sting*).

The people of Hawaii were very excited by the rare chance to watch these stars and the crew make a motion picture.

When the call went out for locals to portray background parts and extras in the movie, Bette Midler was one of the first to answer. Like almost every person who stood in line, auditioned, and filled out forms, she must have had big dreams of so greatly impressing the casting scouts that they would immediately hire her for a big part in their next film. But even landing a small role, as well as the $300 weekly salary that went with it, was probably more than enough to satisfy Bette's need for cash and fantasy.

Bette was chosen to play a missionary's wife, and *Hawaii* would be a great learning experience for her. She would discover just how much hurrying there was, only to then wait for someone or something else. But she would also find a special expression in acting, one that made her know that *this* was what she would have to do in order to be satisfied with her life.

Unfortunately, *Hawaii* was too long. And when it was put together in late 1965 and early 1966, this became glaringly obvious to all who previewed it, so a great deal of the work of many of the actors was cut out. No doubt some of Bette's best scenes were left on a cutting-room floor. Nonetheless, in the versions that were further edited for television, she can be seen playing the part of a miserable, seasick bride to the hilt.

It was ironic that at a time when Bette had had enough of Hawaii, playing an arriving missionary would buy her a ticket out of paradise. The film's producers asked her to return to Los Angeles with them, thinking that they might need her for post-production work. She was guaranteed $300 per week for this as well, and the studio gave her an additional $70 weekly for meals. Deciding to go east was probably one of the easiest decisions Bette ever made.

Yet nothing spectacular happened to Bette in Los Angeles. She did her work, collected her money, pocketed every penny she could scrape together (saving most of it), and looked for opportunities. Funny-looking, short, Jewish women, however, were rarely given a second glance by most casting executives. Hollywood, after all, was the city that picked a blue-eyed blond to play Jesus, and for Bette the Tinseltown of the 1960s appeared to offer little except a closed door.

Looking further east, she packed her bags and moved to New York. There, where the play was the thing, surely she could find a break. On Broadway, after all, looks were not as important as brass, and Bette certainly had a great deal of *that*.

Upon arriving in New York, she checked into the very seedy but very cheap Broadway Central Hotel. The poor surroundings and the loud tenants were not all that different than what she was used to, and Bette was willing to put up with a few inconveniences in order to find her dreams of stardom.

It didn't take long for Bette to discover that parts were few and far between, and the money she had made from *Hawaii* was not going to last long. She took to working whatever jobs she could find just to make ends meet. The future Divine Miss M even worked for a short time as a file clerk at Columbia University.

She worked as a glove salesperson in Stern's department store. (Surely nothing was more ironic than having someone from a tropical paradise help people pick out gloves.) Waiting on people wasn't Bette's strong suit, so it was no surprise when she abruptly quit her job after she and a customer couldn't agree on a choice.

Many other part-time jobs followed and no job was probably more unusual to Bette than a long hitch as a go-go dancer. While it was true that the clubs she worked at catered to men and were hardly the classiest joints in the city, she never had to perform topless nor was she ever asked to provide "extra favors." What she mainly did was dance and smile. Even though it wasn't Broadway, it was showtime. In a way she was a star, and it was far better than any of the other odd jobs she had ever worked at.

As 1965 slowly passed, Bette began to spend her spare nights alternating between two places. One was the public library. This imposing building offered her a wealth of sheet music, records, and books. She had always been an avid reader, but she concentrated on researching the great female stars of other eras. She studied the music style of blues singer Bessie Smith, she discovered the power of black gospel, and she was especially impressed by the unique style and wit of Sophie Tucker.

These influences began to have such a strong effect that they would dramatically change the way Bette appeared at her other after-dark hangouts—New York's small clubs and restaurants. Here she would beg for a chance to perform, usually for no money, and then incorporate what she had studied into her act. Her songs, her vocal style, her jokes—even her clothes—seemed utterly incongruous with the times. When she was reaching back to the forties for a blues number, wrapping herself in long dresses and high heels, the in crowd was listening to rock'n'roll of the British invasion, wearing minis and groovy gear. Bette should have been just as painfully different in these arenas as she had been in Hawaii, yet surprisingly she wasn't.

Her act interested people who saw it. It wasn't polished or slick, and it lacked the consistent style to establish it beyond the small showcases where she was working, but it did show that the woman had power and an instinctive grasp for entertaining. She was an original—unlike anything else most of the club patrons had ever seen, and she definitely wasn't imitating Petula Clark or the Beatles. In 1966, though, there was little money in what she was doing, and seemingly less future.

As the months dragged by, Bette continued to audition. She wanted a part in a musical, to appear on the legitimate stage. As all actresses who parade from call to call, she must have had growing doubts as to whether that would ever happen.

Around her at the hotel were living examples of women who had tried for too long to make it. Many had turned to drugs, and others had supported their habits by resorting to prostitution. For the relative newcomers, these scenes must have been frightening, but they also served to drive determined performers, like Bette, on. For the energetic Miss Midler, lonely nights filled only with cigarettes must have offered her reasons to wonder. Still, she had left a place she had hated, a place where she'd had no future and no hope, and so no matter how bad things were, they couldn't be any worse than they'd been in Hawaii. Bette Midler was going to stick it out.

She was talented, but so were thousands of other New York actresses. She was also lucky. During a casting call for the hit musical *Fiddler on the Roof,* she finally got a callback. With her strong voice and Jewish background, she won a part in the chorus. She couldn't have been happier. The steady job would give her a chance to move to better digs, and the part, no matter how seemingly insignificant, would place her in a position to grow as an actress and meet important people who could help her open the right doors.

With some of her earnings, she enrolled in all kinds of acting, singing, and dancing lessons. Now that she had a break, she needed to make the most of the opportunity, and she worked harder and more than ever.

On off-nights and after shows, Bette continued

to sing at the small clubs, usually being paid next to nothing. And when she wasn't performing, she was learning. With the help of others in the *Fiddler* cast, she explored new musical styles and concepts. She wasn't afraid to expand her act or change it. Unlike most of those around her, she wasn't just concentrating on being a Broadway star. By now she had determined that she would do almost anything to make a living in show business, and her opportunities would not be limited by only considering one option.

As a teen she had loved plays, and she devoted more time to them now. She was particularly impressed with Tom Eyen and his plays such as *Sarah B. Divine!* and *Who Killed My Bald Sister Sophie.* Some people referred to this type of work as belonging to the Theater of the Ridiculous, and Bette was deeply impressed by the irreverent and off-the-wall humor; she incorporated some of it into her nightclub act. She was beginning to use various New York influences to weave something very unique.

After Bette had been in *Fiddler* for about a year, one of the female leads, playing the important role of Tzeitel, the eldest daughter, left the show. She suggested to the director, Jerome Robbins, that he give the part to Bette. A casting woman, who had a friend in mind for the role, bitterly disapproved of this choice, and went to Robbins to attempt to dissuade him. A small war broke out, and even though Bette won the part, her feelings did not escape unscathed. Bette had considered the casting director a friend, and the episode infuriated her. Trust of people—something Bette had never had in copious amounts—would erode further. This lack of trust would haunt her personal and business relationships for years.

For all practical purposes, Bette should have been feeling pretty secure. Less than two years after leaving home, she had secured a coveted role on Broadway, lived in a comfortable apartment, was making a good income, and was in a position to earn even more. She had a number of good friends and relationships . . . yet she wasn't satisfied. She wanted more.

Bette's sister Judy had moved to New York to work, and she offered Bette the support she needed to help her realize just how far she had come and what the future could offer. It was also Judy who helped Bette realize just how much she needed a friend, someone she could trust. For Bette, it was a wonderful feeling to know that her sister was only a short trip away.

When Broadway and her part became too common—after three years in *Fiddler*—and when she began to feel bored with doing the same thing every night, Bette quit. It wasn't the smart or secure thing to do, but it was something that would mark Bette's career for years to come. She liked to do things that were different. Of course, this might mean being hungry again, too, but Bette needed something a bit more spontaneous in her life.

She began to concentrate more and more on her club work. After several months of refining her act and getting nowhere, she hit on something special. Her big break came at the Improvisation on 9th Avenue and 44th Street. It should have been just another gig with a few grins, a chance to try out some material, and no pay for her work. Instead, it was the kickoff to a whole new career.

The owner, Bud Friedman, was used to seeing every bad act in New York, but Bette caught his eye and turned his head. Within this short, flashy girl, he saw something unique. As she worked from her first number into her second, the audience intently listened, something Friedman rarely saw them do for an unknown act. Then, as she began to sing "God Bless the Child," her third number, the crowded club came unglued. Bette herself didn't even know what was happening. She had never felt so much power, so much strength. The roof literally lifted up.

As she continued, every eye in the place focused on her, and everyone in the audience knew that he or she was witnessing something very special. At the end of "God Bless the Child" Bette was screaming, and so was the crowd. With one song, for one moment, she had not been just another unpolished act—she had been a star. The feeling of exhilaration that had built inside her soul fueled her through the rest of her act. Later, Friedman asked if she would like him to manage her.

With Friedman at the helm and the confidence of her performance behind her, Bette began to share her wit and talent not only in small clubs, but on the David Frost and Merv Griffin talk shows as well. She wasn't much more than a novelty yet, but she was reaching more and more people. Still, she wasn't making the money she once had on Broadway, and it seemed that she had a long way to go when it came to attaining real respect and fame. Despite the work, the thought of a new Broadway play appealed to her, although the prospects of landing a part seemed very slim. So she continued to grind it out at small clubs. Who knows what would have happened if she had won a lead in a play at that time—the Divine One might never have been born!

In 1968, as Bette was attempting to further define what type of work she wanted to pursue, tragedy struck. Her sister Judy was walking along a street when a car backed out of an underground garage, striking her and pinning her against a wall. She was hit with such force that her body was severely mangled, almost beyond recognition. Her identification led the police to Bette, and she was called down to the morgue to identify her sister's remains. Then she had to call home and deliver the news to her parents. For most of 1968, Bette would remain in a state of deep depression, attempting to deal with her own career and the loss of her sister. Even with the help of psychoanalysis, it wouldn't come easy. For a long time, New York would be a very lonely place.

In the early spring of 1969, Bette detoured from her solo act when she landed a roll in another musical, *Salvation.* But this musical didn't live up to its name. It closed within days of opening, putting Bette and a host of others back on the streets.

Giving up on Broadway, Bette began to hit the club scene again. Working hard, playing tough, she made enough money to pay her bills and survive, and the next two years were filled with long hours and few rewards. Stardom, even on a local level, eluded Bette. Yet she was making inroads. She managed to entertain thousands watching daytime television with her outrageous off-the-cuff comments on shows hosted by such people as Virginia Graham. She was a great talk-show guest, and this kept her profile up and brought in bookings from small clubs on weekends.

She now had a regular boyfriend, someone who shared her love of music and entertaining. Michael Federal was a guitarist who also sang, and he regularly accompanied Bette on her club dates.

In late 1970, a tour, to areas outside New York, was arranged to see how Ms. Midler would play in midstream America. A novelty, she sang and joked to interested but not very impressive houses on the tour—until she hit the Chicago club, Mr. Kelly's. While opening for Jackie Vernon, she wowed both the patrons and the local press. One writer, Bruce Vilanch of *Chicago Today,* was so impressed with her satirical, off-color wit—and she with him—that he began to write comedy material for her act. This writer/performer arrangement would continue for years.

The reception at Mr. Kelly's gave a boost to Bette's career. She returned to New York with new confidence and some momentum (although, of course, she had both these things before, only to watch them slip away when local club dates didn't work as well). Could she find a place where her unique talents could take hold, expose her to enough people, launch a career beyond that of a lounge-act singer? Those who were betting, were betting no.

3

BETWEEN DATES AND TOURS IN 1970, THINGS WERE slow. Bette had even contemplated a return to go-go dancing in order to make ends meet. She was saved from this fate by a telephone call from Steven Ostrow, the manager of the Continental Baths, which had long been the hot spot for the New York homosexual crowd. It was a place where men would come in, take their clothes off, then wrap themselves in a towel for a steam bath and a trip to a fantasy land that few staid citizens could imagine.

Ostrow had decided that he could increase the number of patrons at his establishment if he remodeled and provided entertainment, so he called in one of New York's best designers and set up a kind of piano bar/lounge on the bottom floor. There the customers could dance, laugh, and take in a variety of musical styles Ostrow brought in to entertain them each weekend.

To secure acts, Ostrow would scout the local dives for up and coming talent. Usually this talent would be hungry enough to work cheap and not be scared off by the club's homosexual label. It was at one of these clubs that he first caught Bette Midler. Bette was—as she usually was—being outrageous. Not only was she singing her campy songs, but she was doing wild takeoffs of every great female entertainer from Sophie Tucker to Martha Raye. She was so overstated that she almost looked like a man doing impressions of a woman. As soon as Ostrow saw her, he knew she would make a big splash at his Baths.

Bette was hungry—not only for money, but for exposure. She quickly accepted Ostrow's offer and results be damned. For the next several weekends, Bette wowed the men with her burlesque-style humor, her divine flare for reshaping old songs, and her outlandish dress. She looked as if she had bought her clothes at a rummage sale, and tossed them on, entirely mismatched, and the audience loved her seemingly total lack of fashion knowledge and style. She was part Mae West, part Charlotte Greenwood, part Joan Davis—but most of all she was all Bette Midler, and she was a hoot.

It was true that Bette was a strange bird who didn't seem to fit into normal society, certainly not with her pedal pushers and animal-skin tops, and her musical taste. Her ideas of classic tunes were "Leader of the Pack" and "Boogie Woogie Bugle Boy." With her hair a bright red and her earthy humor, she was like no woman the men at the Baths had ever known. She was, in a strange sort of way, very close to being what many of them wanted to be . . . different, proud, and showy. Yet they couldn't. With Bette, her energy, and her openness, they could embrace a person who embodied the way they wished things really were.

For Bette, the "tubs," as she called them, were a forum where for fifty bucks a night she could try out her wildest routines, and she felt very much at home there. She loved the energy of the audience, and she also loved their lack of inhibition, due in no small part to the fact that all they had on were their towels. There was a warmth at the Baths that was more than steam. For the struggling entertainer, this was a taste of stardom. It wasn't making her rich, but it was laying a foundation that would make her a cult hero to at least one group of people. At the time she would jokingly say, "The fags love me." And they did.

Her first few weekends at the Baths were great fun and gave Bette a new enthusiasm for another tour. After she completed it, she returned for more gigs and found that Ostrow had recently hired a new piano player. He asked Bette to get together with the young man before her appearance, feeling that this pianist could help the brassy singer polish her act. Ostrow guaranteed that this guy was uniquely talented, too, and his name was Barry Manilow.

Bette and Barry's first meeting didn't go well. He thought her crude and pushy. She smoked too much, was ill-mannered, thought little of anyone but herself, and seemed to believe he should be grateful for the opportunity to work with a star of her magnitude. Barry was a shy and serious man who wrote and arranged very complicated works, and at the time was making good money writing some of the country's best-known commercial jingles. He didn't need the kind of grief that this woman—who acted like a legend, but couldn't read a note of music—was bringing him. Nevertheless, he had to work with her. After all, he was only the piano player.

According to both Bette and Barry, their first few rehearsals together were spent fighting their way through familiar numbers, with neither impressing the other or showing any real energy or interest in doing anything other than getting through each session. Yet on Bette's opening night, the mood and feeling between the two swung full circle.

Bette's first number that evening was "Friends." Manilow was amazed by the energy she displayed when she reached the stage. It was like nothing he had ever seen in rehearsal. She exploded through number after number, each one bringing a frenzied burst of atomic power, each one sending the audience into a storm of towel waving and screaming. She climaxed with "I Shall Be Released," and everyone was. (In his 1987 book, *Sweet Life,* Manilow recalled that he broke three piano strings during the first evening because of his own excitement.) Bette had definitely made a more favorable impression on him.

Evidently, Barry had impressed Bette, too. In her typical fashion, she told him that he was going to be her musical director. And so began one of the strangest teams of all time: a tall, thin, quiet, classically trained, baby-faced pianist who just wanted to play his music and make some money; and a short, dumpy, bizarre, wild-woman, usually dressed in corsets and spiked heels, whose voice was the only thing louder than her outfits. They were Mutt and Jeff, day and night, but the one thing they would never be was boring.

Night after night during the first part of 1971, Bette brought down the house at the Baths. The success of her Andrews Sisters' tunes, dirty jokes, foul language, and takeoffs of Judy Garland, Tallulah Bankhead, and Bette Davis endeared her to the gay community. But she yearned for an even bigger following, so she constantly worked with Manilow on numbers that would show her full musical range and hopefully propel her uptown.

Word soon leaked out about Bette's shows, and newspaper critics began reviewing her strange mixture of songs and humor, claiming that it was so funny and so energetic that everyone should see it—even if it was at "that place." Suddenly, there were as many straights at the Continental Baths as gays; lines of people could be seen waiting to catch her show. A special area for clothed people was even set up. In a campy sort of way, Bette was a smash. Yet she was only taken as seriously as Tiny Tim had been a few years before—as a hot novelty.

Johnny Carson caught one of her shows and asked her to appear on *The Tonight Show,* which was taping in New York at the time. The other networks were challenging him with their nighttime formats, and he and the NBC executives were constantly looking for new blood that would continue to give them the right mix of star power and quirky new acts to stay at the top of the ratings. Bette Midler definitely qualified as quirky.

Her singing style, off-the-wall comments, and constant banter with Carson made her an instant success. A whole new cult following demanded that he have her back, and in a few weeks he did. Over the next several months, she would return seven times.

When she wasn't getting exposure on late-night TV, she was talking to David Frost. And in order to reach a broader audience, she kept looking for something to do in prime time. That something became a special guest appearance on a Burt Bacharach special. No composer in the country was hotter than Bacharach, and Bette's appearance on this top-rated special opened up a large audience ready to see something new and different. Bette, with her trashy style, *was* different, and her renditions of forties' hits *was* something new, too. She appealed to kids through her rebellious personality, but the establishment also liked her music. She had a mixture that meant stardom if the right doors continued to open for her.

In May, she jumped at an offer to play the dual role of Mrs. Walker and the Acid Queen in the Seattle Opera Company's production of the rock musical *Tommy*. This was her first venture into modern rock music, and while it did show off her vocal range and her acting abilities, it also forced her to live by a script. Bette was better suited to inventing her act as she went along, relying on her instincts and the mood of the audience to guide her. As great an experience as Seattle had been, she yearned to be back on the stage in a concert-type format.

With Manilow, she formed a band and hit the road. She worked places that had just a year before thought her only a novelty act; now they were beginning to take her seriously. She toned down her act, doing less off-color material and hoping that middle America would be as taken by her as New York's gay community. The response was encouraging, but not sensational. Just the same, the patrons did turn out, mainly because Bette defied description.

In July, she returned to Mr. Kelly's, once again proving that Chicago loved her outrageousness. She laughed and joked, and carried off top-shelf reviews. However, she and the critics wondered how long she could hold the spotlight as a "camp" performer. When Bette returned to New York, she was ready to do something to prove she had staying power.

In October, she, Manilow, and her band opened to standing-room-only crowds at a club called Downstairs at the Upstairs, where the audience ate up the frenzied, adult entertainment. While it was true that a sizable amount of her audience was gay, she was making some inroads into the establishment, and everyone who watched was carried away by what she did, by her energy, and her unique choice of material and costumes.

It didn't seem to matter if she was singing

"Chapel of Love" or telling an off-color story—the people who had heard about Bette Midler wanted her to do more. At this club, at this moment, she was a star. Rex Reed and other New York critics, while not quite sure what they were seeing, agreed that it was good entertainment.

Her original two-week engagement was stretched to ten weeks, and Bette and her crew continued to pack them in at the West 56th Street club night after night. William Hennessey, who had been her hairdresser a few years before, joined the band as a collaborator. He wrote jokes, came up with new material, and kept the show running smoothly. He also made sure that the right people heard about Bette. Later, he was at least partially responsible for landing a recording opportunity for the young singer. Hennessey was a man Bette would always remember.

As 1971 wound down, Bette found herself wanting to expand the show, build a bigger band, and add more original arrangements. She also was having to fight just to keep Manilow satisfied. Barry wanted out. Working with Bette had been fine, but he was a unique talent. He wanted to write his own material, sing and sell his jingles, and not have to work with a singer who was as moody as Bette was.

While she thrived on hard work, Bette also was a social creature who tried the patience of the much more understated Manilow. Still, he loved and admired her as an entertainer, and every time he tried to leave, she sweetly convinced him that she needed him for a few more months, and *then* he could go. Those few months eventually turned into a few years.

In 1972, she was back at the Baths for a "farewell appearance." She had already done about a dozen such-labeled appearances, but the audiences knew that these February shows might truly be the last. She was becoming a local legend, and her successful engagement at Downstairs at the Upstairs had proven that she could bring in patrons at a club that catered to something other than gays. Her dollar value was soon going to price her out of her original place of recognition; on many nights during these last shows, the straights outnumbered the gays. The people who had discovered her and made her a local star were being pushed aside by her new fans. Bette was in.

Rex Reed, reviewing her last shows at the Baths, spoke glowingly of not only her performances but her future. He became one of the first to state that Ms. Midler might actually have staying power. Another who thought so was Johnny Carson.

Bette's seven appearances on Carson's show had introduced her to the entire country, although they really didn't have the effect on her career that another Carson invitation would. Carson was working the Sahara in Las Vegas in April and needed an opening act. He had become so enamored with Bette, and he was so convinced that her one-of-a-kind routine would play well with the gamblers who had paid big bucks to see his show, that he asked her to open for him. Working up a larger show, which now included a bigger band and a female backup group known as the Harlettes (one white girl surrounded by two blacks—Bette's version of a singing Oreo cookie), she hit the Strip.

Johnny had been right: Vegas loved Midler. They laughed at her jokes, applauded her singing, and were wowed by her many different characters and outfits. However, despite the good reviews, Bette wondered if she was really up to par. At the Baths, the men had waved their towels, jumped onstage and danced with her, asked her to make love to them, and screamed for her to do more. In Vegas, the finely dressed crowd had stood when her show was over, but they never became involved in the action. After New York, these crowds seemed a little bit dead.

Vegas was also a place where being outlandish didn't really make a person stand out. In and around the gambling Strip, a person was practically ignored even if nude, and being flashy and trashy seemed to make Bette fit in *more*. Vegas became an experience that paid big bucks and put her name in big bright lights, but it wasn't a milestone of personal accomplishment. If anything, it may have made Bette wonder if she wasn't running out of steam. Nonetheless, she continued to play all her tricks, making the audience laugh by introducing the Harlettes, one of whom was a pretty, fair singer named Melissa Manchester, as "New York's three biggest sluts," and her band members as drug addicts.

A truckful of big-time money, a month of hard work, and great reviews from the local and national press still left a lingering question about whether Bette's act was one destined for national success, or more likely resembling a comet streaking across a nighttime sky. After all, many people had successfully played Vegas, only to flop when they tried Peoria.

What Bette's career needed was a shot in the arm, something to dramatically introduce her unique style to the masses who didn't go to nightclubs or casinos. Carson had helped—but her appearances on his show hadn't really positioned her to be taken seriously. What would?

4

NINETEEN-SEVENTY-TWO WOULD BECOME A PIVOTAL year for Bette Midler. When she had worked at Downstairs at the Upstairs the year before, she had attracted scores of critics, hundreds of patrons, and one other special man: Ahmet Ertegun. Ertegun was the so-called Sultan of the Pop World, and as president of Atlantic Records had made many so-so talents into big-name stars. Ertegun had been so impressed with Bette's performance that he immediately approached her about a recording contract. As he would later say when looking back at that night, "She was overwhelming. I couldn't believe that a young person like her could not only understand those old musical styles so well, but capture so accurately the flavor of the period. And it was extraordinary how she could take all the styles and make them a part of herself. It was the wittiest musical performance I'd ever seen." The fact that the audience was the most enthusiastic that New York had seen in years must also have helped convince him of Bette's marketability.

At the time of the record executive's offer, Bette was living in a one-bedroom garden apartment in Greenwich Village. She was still poor by normal entertainment standards, but far above where she had been a few years before when living in cheap hotel rooms and go-go dancing for a living. Determined to be a big star, Bette must have felt as though she were only one break away. . . . Perhaps Ertegun's offer was the one that would do it.

Atlantic now had this incredible live performer, and promptly released a flurry of press releases outlining its plans to capture her raw talents and make her a superstar. Yet within a matter of weeks, the company discovered that it didn't have any idea of what to do with her. Everything that she was—all that made her special—seemed to be experienced best in a concert setting, and coming up with a way to put this person and her performance on vinyl would take a great deal of work and planning. The label turned to one of its most successful producers, Joel Dorn, to capture the exuberance of Bette.

At first glance it didn't seem that difficult. After all, Bette had a great voice, a large regional following, and was already using some of Manilow's super arrangements of wonderful old tunes. She definitely had a style, and she was unique.

Dorn took in one of Bette's shows, and then, caught up in the rapture of the moment, announced that he could and would give her a magnificent album—maybe the best he'd ever done. It was not hard to become so enthused. At the end of Bette's final set, the patrons were literally standing on the tables screaming, begging for more.

Bette was thrilled that Dorn, the man who had just produced Roberta Flack's Grammy-winning album, would be working with her. Taking the arrangements she had used in her show—the arrangements for which Manilow had been primarily responsible—he set to work on capturing that special Midler sound. But it wasn't a smooth transition. As a matter of fact, it became a nightmare.

From day one, things just weren't right. Dorn was doing a good job of capturing the singer's voice, but her drive and fire seemed to be lost in the arrangements and instrumentation. The playbacks sounded more like Bette Midler doing Roberta Flack versions of Bette Midler songs. It was too smooth. Bette's music had always been right on the edge, just a breath away from falling over the brink.

For a while, even Bette didn't realize that the sessions weren't coming out successfully. But those close to her, the musicians who normally worked with her—especially Manilow—felt that Atlantic was selling the performer short. The songs were the same ones that people loved in clubs, but the new arrangements seemed to all but overshadow the singer so that she sounded just like everybody else. Worse, she sounded like that while singing songs from a different era. What hope did she have of scoring on the charts? Most of those who knew Bette believed that the record would flop, and that the singer's career would be hindered greatly by that failure.

Several months after seeing her show, Ahmet Ertegun heard a rough cut of the album. It would be an understatement to say that he was disappointed. This boring material had been recorded by what he considered a can't-miss artist. Not only that, it had been produced by his best producer. Yet, even after meeting after meeting and reworking the material with new sessions, the results were only slightly better. Months had now passed, and by this time, Ertegun realized that he couldn't release the album as it was.

The press had gotten wind of the troubles at Atlantic, and the reports in New York media indicated two things. First (and correctly), the rumor mill pumped out the news that the record was not very good, and that Bette's critics and fans would be disappointed when it was released. Secondly (and falsely), many releases stated that one of the problems during the recording sessions was that Bette was being difficult. It was true that Bette was often hard to work with, but not in this case. She had done everything that Dorn and the others had asked, and the fact that the album wasn't very good was hardly her fault.

Trying to forget the problems at the studio, Bette and Manilow worked tirelessly on what both of them felt was the most important engagement of Bette's performing career: Carnegie Hall. In what was to become a typical New York reaction to the news that Ms. Midler was giving a concert, the fabled facility was completely sold out within hours of the announcement of the show. This response put even more pressure on Midler and Manilow to squeeze everything they could from their music.

Hours and hours of long rehearsals were staged, and the pressure soon began to take its toll. Name-calling, arguments, and actual fights broke out as the group struggled to perfect what had been less than a year in the making—a show that would bring to the world the real Divine Miss M. It had to be better than the club shows because at Carnegie Hall, the music and the staging would make this performance fly, not Bette's raw jokes or humor. At Manilow's insistence, Bette even hired an orchestra for the event.

Uncharacteristically, Bette was extremely nervous before the show, and so was her band. How would this audience, dressed so nicely and sitting in such comfortable seats, respond to her show? What would happen to the show's energy if the crowd just politely sat there, waiting for the music and excitement to come to them? What if Bette failed to bring this hallowed stage to life, and the once-friendly critics panned her show? What if she did the unthinkable—and flopped?

At curtain time, a shaky Bette stormed onstage, grinned at the audience, took a deep breath to calm her nerves, and then literally exploded with energy and talent. Never had she been so good or so talented or so wound up. Bette had never been so on—so right, and even the orchestra got caught up in her energy. Very staid musicians were bouncing to the beat of a very different drummer.

That night's show would have become a fading

memory to all of those who performed and watched if someone had not made a bootleg tape and sold it to Barry Manilow. Manilow's only reason for buying the tape was to enshrine his night as the conductor at Carnegie Hall. He had never planned to allow anyone outside of his own family to ever hear it. But it would become something more, something so special that it would help launch both Bette and himself into recording fame.

While Manilow kept his secret, listening to it over and over again, the executives at Atlantic had decided that Bette's current album simply wouldn't sell in its present form, and with hundreds of hours and several months invested in it, they were beginning to question if Ms. Midler could really ever succeed as a recording artist. They were very close to giving up.

How ironic. The songs that had gone over so well at the Carnegie Hall concert had fallen flat on Atlantic recording tape. Even though something had to be done, what else could be tried? Atlantic's rejection of her material left Bette flat at a time when she should have been sky-high. She was completely demoralized. To cheer her up, Manilow invited her to his place and let her listen to his tape of their Carnegie Hall performance. The tape blew her away while restoring her self-confidence. She knew she was good—she could *hear* it.

Letting the moment seize them, Manilow and Bette took the tape to Ertegun's office and asked him to listen to it. Suddenly, the reason that the executive had been so impressed with Bette, as well as the reason he had signed her over six months before, came back to him. That was the sound he had heard and wanted. Ertegun quickly asked Manilow if he had ever produced an album, and Manilow lied and said he had. Ertegun immediately gave Manilow the project, and Bette's recording career was on its way to being saved.

Everything changed, beginning with the way the music was recorded. Unlike Dorn, who had used studio musicians, Manilow used Bette's band and laid down all the tracks simultaneously in order to interject life into the project. The sessions were now fun, energetic, and dynamic. They had a raw edge, but still sounded polished. Central in Manilow's mind was Bette's voice. He highlighted and pushed it out in front of everything else, and supported it with the instruments. His methods worked and within days, an album that had taken almost half-a-year and gone nowhere was suddenly completed.

As Atlantic pressed the album, worked up publicity, and began to define where and how it would market this unique singer, Bette, Barry, and the band hit the road again. They played exotic places like Rochester, Toronto, Boston, Los Angeles, the Southwest, and almost anywhere else that would pay them. While in Canada, Bette even took time out to play a small part in a low-budget picture entitled *A Story Too Often Told.* This foray into film would later embarrass her, but for now, Bette simply thought it was fun to portray Mary in a satirical sendup of the story of Jesus. She never dreamed it might come back to haunt her. After all, it was just a few hours and a bit part.

Having broken up with her last boyfriend, though,

Bette, now nearing thirty, was not only growing weary of the road and her heavy schedule—after all, she had been working constantly for several years—but she was tired of being alone. At this point, a twenty-nine-year-old ex-rock'n'roll producer/ nightclub owner entered her life.

Aaron Russo first heard of Bette in Chicago, a city that had fallen head over heels for her on her initial visits some years before. Russo was a chunky dynamo—certainly no hunk—yet something must have attracted Bette to this man at their initial meeting. Many believed that it may have been his sense of humor or his unique style of dress, or perhaps his boldness. Yet some said that it was probably something far simpler—Russo's belief that Bette could be a big star.

He had arranged a meeting with the singer through a mutual friend, and at that first meeting told Bette that he had lobbied hard two years before for a friend of his at a major record label to sign her to a long-term contract. Whether this was an exaggeration or not, it impressed Bette.

Even Russo must have been a bit taken aback when she told him that she didn't want to be just a star—she wanted to be a legend. He rose to the bait, and said he could help make her one. He began to fill her head with plans for movies, world-wide tours, and awards. Why be satisfied with being the toast of New York when she could be the queen of the world? And it wouldn't be that hard—he could do it for her.

Russo would become to Bette what no one else ever had: a dominating force. For the next six months, their business and love lives would be one. And he would make her every decision for the next seven years. He paid her bills, arranged her travel, and saw that her personal needs were taken care of. He answered her mail, returned calls, and kept her at arm's length from the people he felt were too important or not important enough for her to meet. He even tried to control the people she wanted as friends. He literally ran her life.

Many people questioned how much business Russo had managing her. While he had produced shows for some of the really big acts of the time, he wasn't near the name he claimed to be. He was a concert and club promoter, not a single-act manager. Just the same, he became to her what Colonel Tom Parker had been to Elvis—the all-knowing force behind the star. Of course, there has always been some real question as to just how much responsibility he had for her success. Many feel he may have held her back.

When Russo touched base with Bette, she was already hot in certain circles, and the groundwork had been laid for her to ascend into other arenas, such as film. Manilow had been responsible for her early recording success. In retrospect, if Aaron Russo can be given credit for anything, it would be a sense of direction and organization. Up until the time that Russo entered her life, Bette had been a bundle of energy, but was headed in a multitude of directions. Now, with Russo as the navigator, that energy was channeled.

Russo began to negotiate new club dates for Bette, and one of the biggest he put together was a

New Year's Eve gig at Lincoln Center. There, Manilow and Bette, together for one of their last shows, put on a performance that brought the house down. She had wanted to make this show something special to remember, so as a joke she had planned to tape marijuana joints under each of Lincoln Center's 3,000 seats, and then invite the audience to light up at midnight. Her attorney and Russo had convinced her that this would not be in her best interest. So Bette worked on another plan . . . a real big pair of surprises.

Her show that night was typical Bette. Initially she had marched onstage in a big diaper to represent the new year. After that unique opening, she changed, did her songs, most of them off the just-released album, and of course did the raunchy jokes her fans loved. But the best was saved for last. At the midnight hour, in front of a crowd that wanted to party all night long, Bette released a hook, letting the top of her dress fall to her waist to reveal two of the biggest uncovered and previously unknown facets of the entertainer . . . her bare breasts. As the critics would remark, "What a way to welcome the new year." Smiling, Bette had made a clean breast to begin the new year. But that was just the beginning.

As 1973 rolled in, Bette kicked Russo out of her bed while still retaining him as her manager. Their relationship was now more than a bit strained, but Russo, doing his job and fielding both movie offers and club dates, managed to stay in control of everything outside the bedroom. Tensions eased considerably with the release of the album *The*

Divine Miss M. Almost every reviewer across the country loved it. The first single, "Do You Want to Dance?"hit the charts on January 20, stayed there for eleven weeks, and peaked at number seventeen.

In June, Bette had a legitimate top-ten record. "Boogie Woogie Bugle Boy," the Andrews Sisters' hit of World War II, peaked at number eight, and her album was now riding the top of the charts. Atlantic wanted her in the studio again with Manilow, and the only reason it took a while to get them there was that Barry was almost as hot as Bette. He was working on an album of his own, and his studio was pushing him to get something out quickly.

Meanwhile, Bette moved on, toured the country again, said hello to Johnny Carson, and returned home for a Hawaii show and a class reunion. Suddenly, the high school classmates who had once thought her so strange now wanted to have their picture taken with her. For Bette, time was a healer that proved she was going to come out on top. The return home was a wonderful experience of redemption. If there was a blot on the Hawaiian trip, though, it was that her father had refused to come and see her show. But her mother had been there and loved it.

Right after the tour, Russo and ABC announced that Bette would do a television special for the network in the fall of that year. The official release said that the network couldn't wait to expose Bette's multitude of talent. It was an exposure that would never come. Negotiations about the nature and the content of the special would eventually break down, and even though Bette and ABC would talk for the next few years, the show was never made.

The Divine Miss M was making Bette a star of the airwaves and record sales. And then Bette would take home the Grammy for Best New Female Artist. The woman who would present Bette with the award was Karen Carpenter, a superstar who represented the opposite side of the industry. As the two stood side by side—a thin, quiet singer and a short, brash, energetic entertainer; Karen, all-American in looks and manners and Bette, all-back-alley—few would have predicted that the best days for Karen Carpenter were behind her, and the best days for Bette Midler still lay ahead.

5

WITH A TREMENDOUS YEAR BEHIND HER, BETTE WAS riding a crest of popularity that should have been exploited for all it was worth. There were millions of dollars waiting to be made, and hundreds of different opportunities staring her in the face. She had won a Grammy, and in an honor even more prestigious, had taken time out to pick up an Antoinette Perry (Tony) Award for Best Special Performance in a Broadway musical.

Her second album, *Bette Midler,* was doing very good business. She had charted again with a single, "Friends," and was assured of even greater things if she would just hit the studio again. Hollywood was calling. Robert Altman wanted her to star in his movie *Nashville.* ABC was still trying to bring her to television, and Broadway producers were trying to reach Aaron Russo on a daily basis. The world was waiting to see what move Bette would make.

Back in Greenwich Village, still occupying the same one-bedroom apartment she had for years, Bette was content to listen to Aretha Franklin albums and spend hours reading biographies of famous women. She simply didn't want to talk about work, much less consider doing any. She was completely burned out.

Some blamed Barry Manilow for her lack of desire and direction. He had hit number one with his first single, "Mandy," and he no longer had time to help Bette discover new music and new arrangements. She had fed off Manilow's drive and creativity.

Others thought that Aaron Russo, who now controlled every career move she made, was the problem. While their love affair had ended, his influence over her life had not diminished. He actually thought for her in almost every facet of business. She seemingly could do little without his input. Her friends began to believe this control had zapped Bette of her energy and desire. Perhaps they were right; whenever Bette had been controlled by circumstances, individuals, or even entertainment vehicles, she had withdrawn into herself and lost her spontaneity.

But perhaps the best explanation for Bette's lack of desire to exploit her wave of success was simply that she had experienced so much of it in such a short amount of time. Suddenly she was not hungry, money was no problem, almost everyone knew her name, and everybody seemed to want her. After ten years of professional struggle—as well as a lifetime of *personal* struggle—she was finally being accepted and embraced. It would hardly be surprising to stop and enjoy the fruits of her labor, or to be overcome by newfound celebrity status.

To escape New York and the constant deluge of new offers and opportunities, Bette headed for the island of Grenada to enjoy the ocean and tropical weather that had been so much a part of her youth. It was time to let other people wait on her, and let other things entertain her. She wanted to enjoy long hours of sleep, quiet evenings with no loud music, and the solitude of long walks in places where no one knew her.

When she tired of Grenada, she went to Honolulu to visit her family. She asked for and received no publicity, and spent most of her time sharing her experiences with her mother.

After Hawaii came France. In a brief period of time she had moved from paradise to the country where love blooms on every corner. She found her share of interesting men, as well as wonderful hours spent in museums, cathedrals, and gardens. She enjoyed the food, the art, and the men equally. But regardless of months of adventure in and around Paris, Bette still didn't seem to have a desire to return to work.

One of the reasons for this lack of desire was that Bette had plenty of cash. She was very careful with a buck, and had bought little with what she had earned. She lived simply, didn't spend money on anything she didn't need, and watched pennies in almost every area of her life. Certainly, part of this came from growing up so very poor, but most of this thriftiness came from a personality that was cautious by nature.

She might have continued to roam Europe for some time if one of her long-forgotten decisions hadn't come back to haunt her. The cheap film she had made some years before in Canada, *A Story Too Often Told,* had been released in New York. Despite the fact that she was seen in only eight minutes of film, she was being labeled as the star of the feature. The title had even been changed to *The Divine Mrs. J.* Suddenly, the fact that the movie poked fun at Christian concepts and Christ himself created a great deal of negative publicity, and it was probably the type of publicity that would hurt Bette dearly in Middle America.

Bette and Aaron Russo had been growing further and further apart, and most felt that they were close to parting when *A Story Too Often Told* hit New York. Acting in Bette's interest, and seeing a potential land mine landing in the middle of her career, Russo picketed the theater showing the film, released countless memos on the exploitative nature of the movie, and quickly turned the New York press against both the movie and its makers. He single-handedly disarmed the land mine, destroyed its credibility, and may have saved Bette's career by doing so.

Bette was grateful, and when she returned from Paris, she and Russo once again came to a solid business arrangement. This actually may have disappointed Russo, for many times he had publicly professed his deep love for Bette. Even though their relationship never again became intimate,

Russo at least had his job securely in hand, and Bette back in New York.

As 1974 wound down and 1975 began, Bette started to weigh her options. She and Russo studied the film proposals, including one in which she would play Janis Joplin in a movie entitled *The Pearl.* But none of the properties really interested either of them. They also picked up talks with ABC, but nothing that satisfied Bette could be worked out. Finally, they considered several offers from Las Vegas. Financially, these were extremely tempting, but Bette's memories of how lukewarm the crowds were convinced her to turn them down.

There were really only two other options. Bette could tour the country or she could try to find a way to return to Broadway. Remembering her exhausting final tour, she opted to return to the stage. The problem was finding the right vehicle.

Bette didn't like any of the shows that producers were offering her; the roles were too restricting. She wanted to do a one-woman show, something with a stylish flair, lots of energy and humor, off-the-wall but with great music. It had to be "trash with flash." What she and Russo came up with was *Clams on the Halfshell Revue.*

They reserved the Minskoff Theater for ten weeks starting in April, and then set about working out the details of who would direct, produce, and star with Bette. The latter was easy. It would be Bette's band, the Harlettes, and a musical legend, Lionel Hampton.

For Hampton, who was celebrating his fortieth year in show business, it would be his first stint on Broadway. He had played everywhere else, worked for five presidents, done dozens of films and television shows, written and sold countless tunes, and had earned the title of Vibes President U.S.A. He was the best at what he did, and just like Bette he was an original.

Russo himself would produce the three hours of entertainment, and helping him was Ron Delsener. These two would demand that their backers put forth hundreds of thousands of dollars even before a news release was issued on the project. To ensure that the money was available—and that investors would be convinced that this would be a huge hit—Russo and Delsener hired two other noted Broadway pros to help them secure a sense of stability, director Joe Layton and set designer Tony Walton.

Walton had a list of credits as long as a Broadway curtain. He had worked with Bob Fosse and had done films like *Mary Poppins* and *Murder on the Orient Express*. Layton was almost a living legend. He had earned a number of Tonys, as well as an Emmy for Streisand's television special, *My Name is Barbra.* With Bette and Lionel, these two made a can't-miss team.

In February, Russo issued the following statement: "Rather than tour the country's huge arenas such as Madison Square Garden for astronomical fees, which she had been offered, Bette has chosen this milieu to best present her art to her fans. For this show, we have surrounded Bette with the ultimate in creative production values. To my knowledge, no artist has ever gone to these lengths or this expense for a limited-run engagement."

Part of Russo's statement was pure hype. Press agents tended to state that their latest offering was going to greater lengths than ever before. Still, *Clams* was spending a great deal of money, and it would be a Midler vehicle unlike any live concert. The only questions were whether Bette could charm Broadway again after such a long layoff, and whether she could hit her musical stride without Manilow and his strong direction.

The day tickets went on sale, over $200,000-worth were sold. Bette was a financial hit a full two months before opening. But what about the critics? After months of work and tremendous personal input, Bette found out just hours after her first performance on April 14.

Rex Reed stated, "Divine Bette Midler—I Love You." *Newsweek* started its review with these words: "At long last a truly exciting musical." Richard Goldstein of the *Village Voice* called Bette's show "intelligent and provocative entertainment. . . . She's at the peak of her musical authority." Emory Lewis said, "It is pure joy—she reminds me of Charlie Chaplin's Little Tramp . . . most brilliant show of her career . . . a glow of love sweeps the audience . . . I suggest that you rush to the box office." And the fans did. Night after night the show sold out.

As crazy as the critics were for Bette's work, the audience loved it even more. They would come to their feet, applause interrupting number after number, and laughter ringing not only during the show but in the lobby as people filed out. New York was alive with the talk of Ms. Midler's return. For Bette it couldn't have been sweeter.

Clams was her baby. She had conceived it, and it had refueled her creative juices. She was once again excited about her work and her career, and she was carrying out one of her own dreams from start to finish. Now she knew that she could be successful and creative without Manilow, and without compromising her own ideas and talent. She was no longer just a flash in the pan or overnight success. She was *legit.*

To understand just how much of Bette went into *Clams,* you only need look at the performance itself. It opened with the overture from another successful musical, *Oklahoma.* Then, when the curtain rose, the audience was greeted with blackfaced actors singing a rockin' version of "Old Man River." Bette entered inside a large clam shell, and jumped out, stating, "I hope you enjoy this because we have busted our buns for y'all." Then she worked hard to prove it.

Over the course of the next 180 minutes, Bette saluted and made fun of almost every classic moment and entertainer in the business. She was a bomb exploding into a thousand different personalities and concepts. Her act unraveled to reveal more and more talent; she smoked with passion, blazed with charm, rolled with humor, and sang with unequaled energy.

She and the Harlettes chewed gum and issued a host of off-color puns. Then, grabbing center stage, she proceeded to tell the audience of her upcoming porno flick, *Temple Emmanuelle*—the story of a horny Jewish girl always on the make. From there she portrayed a slightly less-than-pure Joan of Arc, and finally a zany Fay Wray in the clutches of King Kong. In between these nutsy routines she performed gospel, blues, and big-band numbers.

Somehow in this machine-gun-paced performance she found time to do sendups of Streisand, Minnelli, Joplin, Mae West, Tiny Tim, Don Rickles, Bea Little, Tina Turner, and her idol, Sophie Tucker. Finally, when it seemed that there was no one left to pick on, she did wonderful arrangements of Billie Holiday and Dorothy Lamour tunes.

By the time the show ended, she was ablaze, a goddess of talent and unique charm. In the course of a few weeks, she sold almost $2 million-worth of tickets, broke all house records, and grabbed more press than any entertainer in New York. She was hotter than she had been before she had taken her fifteen-month sabbatical. She, along with Russo, was also in control of her life.

She was so successful that by this time, as she prepared for another concert tour, many of those close to her were wondering if she was going to change—if she was going to take on a spoiled-star personality. Some of these fears seemed to come true when Bette hired a full-time, live-in male secretary. She also seemed to become more serious, taking far less time to socialize with her old friends and more time to be with show business friends. Was success spoiling Bette?

At least part of this question was answered when Bette volunteered to appear on a telethon for the United Jewish Appeal. She gladly appeared at rehearsals, gave freely of her time, didn't demand anything special, and sang not one token number, but four long songs. She talked to callers and the audience, and spent a great deal of time appealing for more money for this worthy cause. And to any who had doubted that she was still the same Bette, she offered one more bit of evidence that she hadn't really changed.

When she was disappointed by the lack of actual pledge responses that her performance had generated, she offered even more of herself. She stated, on the air, that if someone would give $5,000, she would pull her dress off on television. When a caller pledged the amount, Bette unzipped, stepped out, and left the stage clad only in a slip. Everyone went wild, and the act proved that the old Bette was still alive and well in New York. She didn't take her stardom too seriously.

Yet hanging onto old values was becoming harder and harder. Bette was lonely. Everything was happening so fast, and everyone was demanding so much . . . would it ever be possible to truly be loved or have time for a real, long-term relationship?

A part of the little girl who could never do enough to satisfy her friends or her family still lived inside Bette's heart. She wanted a place where she really belonged, and she no doubt wanted someone to belong to. In a way, the fame that she had worked so hard to create ended up keeping her at arm's length from the real world she enjoyed so much. She openly stated that she wanted a family, and she also openly confessed that there was no one special man in her life. In most of her interviews, she spoke of the simple things she enjoyed, like working in the garden and reading. Yet these seemed at such odds with the woman who was so hilariously vulgar as a performer.

As she packed hundreds of great reviews away in her memory, as she gladly accepted an almost legendary status, and as she enjoyed the money she'd earned, she was still unique, alone, and unable to fit into any permanent niche. Despite almost unparalleled success, as Barry Manilow said of her, "She was the most insecure person in the world."

AFTER HER SUCCESS ON BROADWAY IN *CLAMS ON THE Halfshell,* Bette should have been ready to explode into the second half of the 1970s with a furor. But once again what *should* have happened and what *actually* resulted were two different things.

After a successful number of musical dates, Bette finally put together a contract and then a show for television—not with ABC, with whom she had been negotiating for several years, but with the new and inventive Home Box Office. HBO was a division of the conservative Time/Life Corporation, and hardly seemed the type to welcome Miss Notorious to their family. But they needed an unusual talent to begin their new series, *Standing Room Only*.

SRO was supposed to resemble a live concert in a way that no other show of its type ever had. This would be shown as it happened (on tape), without editing, redubbing, or commercials. The viewers were meant to be able to sit in their living room, turn up the sound, and feel as if they were really there. By now, ten years after the debut of such a process, most television viewers know that while televised concerts are good, they can't compare to the real experience. In 1976, however, this surreal advertising concept sold, and it helped HBO pick up a number of first-time premium-cable subscribers.

Bette was probably a great choice for a debut act. Her music seemed to appeal to almost every segment of culture, and she would be something unique and unseen on television. Bruce Vilanch and Jerry Blatt were hired as writers for the show. Vilanch had been close to Bette for almost a decade, having reviewed one of her first Chicago performances, and he knew her almost as well as he knew himself. Combining her ideas with their own talent, the writers provided Bette with a number of super, slightly off-color, and very topical one-liners. The musical part of the show would be composed of much of the same material that she had been doing since her days at the Continental Baths in New York.

The concert was taped at the Cleveland Music Hall over a three-day period in late spring, and then it was edited down to two hours and nineteen minutes for airing in late June. All of the shows were sold out, and the live crowd was very enthusiastic.

As it aired on HBO, Bette opened the show singing underneath the covers of a hospital bed, and then jumped into "You've Got to Have Friends." It was obvious from the number of subscriptions sold by cable companies around the country—due in large part to her show—that she had a whole bunch of friends, or at least curious acquaintances. But what would mom, dad, and the kids think of Ms. Midler's brand of humor?

A good portion of audiences in Middle America—those who had gotten to know Bette on the Carson show—must have been shocked when she began to utter a number of oaths almost always proceeded with s—— or f——. Then, when she began to sing about a "tall" dentist, vocalizing that the man "thrilled her when he drilled her," a number of sets probably were flipped off in shock. But most likely, more were left on as Bette continued to do wild imitations of well-known network television and movie staples such as Arlene Francis and Shelley Winters. When she closed the show dressed as Miss Liberty in a mock bicentennial salute, those who'd stayed tuned were probably grinning from ear to ear and charmed clear down to their toes. The reviewers were, anyway. Even those who didn't like it certainly talked about it.

"She is a phenomenon," stated George Maksian in the New York *Daily News*. He went on to conclude, "She may call herself the last of the tacky women, but we call her sensational." Most other major reviewers agreed. When the showings were over, HBO had proven wise in their choice of the amazing redhead as their first major concert presentation. Their only problem was that she would be a hard act to follow.

Meanwhile, Bette was ready to jump into film

work. She had turned down *Nashville* without a great deal of thought, deciding it simply wasn't suited for her. She and Aaron Russo wanted dearly to find a major starring role that she could use to propel herself into legendary status. Broadway and cable were nice, concert tours made big dollars, and the New York club scene was fun, but Hollywood made the stars that all of America loved.

One of the parts that Bette was offered, only to have Russo turn it down, was opposite Warren Beatty and Jack Nicholson in *The Fortune.* Mike Nichols was directing the film and he badly wanted Bette, but Russo didn't like the part. That proved fortunate, because the movie bombed. Russo had also told Bette to turn down the part of Rocky Balboa's wife in the first *Rocky* film. It might have been interesting to have seen those results.

One part did jump out as something Russo wanted very badly for Bette, and he went after this one—a starring role in Ross Hunter's *Little Me.* Ironically, it was probably Bette's mouth that cost her a chance for this film. She had been thrown out of a theater for laughing at another Ross Hunter film, *Lost Her Reason,* and then she had insulted his remake of *Lost Horizon.* Those two incidents had not gone unnoticed by the famous director, and Bette had been placed on his blacklist. Hunter hired Goldie Hawn instead, and in the process thumbed his nose at Bette and Russo.

Having been unable to work on a film, and not really wanting to jump into mainstream Broadway, even though there had been scores of offers, including the lead in *Mack and Mabel,* Bette returned to recording and touring. The tours were successful; the recording was a different matter.

Her new album, the first in over two years, was also the first without the direction of Barry Manilow. *Tales of a New Depression* should have scored big and placed Bette at the top of charts once more. It didn't. As a matter of fact and public embarrassment, it flopped very badly, both with critics and fans. Many things were blamed, including the inescapable fact that many AM stations (at the time the main source for popular music) considered Bette "camp" and not worthy of their playlists. But the main reason was probably that the recording wasn't very good. It should have been. Some of the best and most respected musicians in the business had taken part; in the studio with Bette were Todd Rundgren, Gotham, Rick Derringer, the Becker Brothers, and even the reclusive Bob Dylan. (An attempt to show the closeness between Dylan and Midler can be heard in a bit of studio dialogue between the two that was left at the end of one of the cuts.) But it just didn't play well. Certainly the songwriting of Tom Waits and Phoebe Snow was not subpar, but, despite the superior musicians, the music didn't have much life. Bette's voice and styling were far from what had earned her the standing ovations during her live shows.

It simply wasn't Bette being Bette. She had been given the opportunity to sing jazz, folk, rock, pop, and reggae, and none of these styles seemed to excite her. The album was basically the very same mistake that had almost been made on her first album. This time there was no Barry Manilow to correct it before it was released. Aaron Russo, genuinely embarrassed, let the press and fans know that the next album would show the real Bette again.

To make matters worse, Bette was not feeling well, and finally entered a hospital near the end of the year. Doctors removed her appendix, and she was released and back in form soon enough to perform her show at the Dorothy Chandler Pavillion in Los Angeles on New Year's Eve. Wanting to make it a very special "blowout," she once more obtained 1,500 joints and ordered her band to tape them under the building's chairs. Before the deed could be done, the Los Angeles District Attorney's office visited with the singer and the crew and convinced them to destroy their joke. Bette was lucky not to have been arrested.

Even without the prank, the concert went very well, and just before the curtain came down, Bette, remembering another old trick, dropped the top of her dress for the crowd. She was greeted by a large, collective gasp, and then a tremendous round of applause. Aaron Russo, standing backstage, quickly dropped the curtain, furious that his star had insisted on ending her show by giving the audience a "booby prize." And Russo wasn't the only person who was not impressed.

Several executives from the RKO radio stations had been in the audience and visited Bette after the show. When she asked them what they'd thought of her act and her new album, they honestly told her that they didn't think much of either. Grabbing an album, Bette smashed it over the head of one of the executives, uttered several oaths, and marched off. RKO struck back by banning Bette Midler records on their stations. In a brief moment of rage, the singer had lost some of the most lucrative radio markets in the country. She had also put herself at odds with her manager.

This type of performance, however, was just what the boys at Harvard were looking for in a star. When they announced the winner of their annual Hasty Pudding Award for Woman of the Year, Bette was far and away their best choice for 1976.

The Harvard award, an irreverent slap in the face, much the same as Bette's performances, was made to order for her. Here was a group of men who didn't take themselves very seriously, and Bette loved that. They paraded her across campus in an old Rolls Royce, and then announced the reasons for their choice before a group of students and press: "This award is being given to that woman who in the last year has demonstrated great artistic skill and feminine qualities. She was the unanimous choice for this award: Her outstanding and innovative approach to singing has made her concerts vibrant and touching theatrical performances."

The local producer of Harvard satirical sendups, Samuel S. Weiss, went so far as to remark that the award has "never before gone to a woman whose style is so close to that of the Pudding." He felt that her shows were in the mold of Pudding's all-male-cast presentations. With these embraces of the outrageous, Bette was in heaven.

Back home, Russo and Bette were battling again,

and jealousy may have been at least a part of the reason. Bette was now living with a stage actor named Peter Reigert, whom she'd met in Chicago in October of 1976. She had gone backstage after a play to visit with her close friend, F. Murray Abraham, who had introduced them. Reigert was from the Bronx and had formerly been a schoolteacher, a social worker, and an advance man for Bella Abzug. Like Bette, he loved to read, and disdained public life beyond his own career. By early 1977 Reigert was starring in the off-Broadway hit *Sexual Perversity in Chicago,* but was probably better known for his nude poster advertising the play. Bette and her friends made regular trips to the Cherry Lane Theater to watch the show and applaud Peter, and it didn't take an eagle eye to understand just what she saw in him.

Russo, trying to separate business from his personal feelings, opted for network television as Bette's next project. He wanted a major, one-woman special, but his first step was booking Bette as a guest star on a Bing Crosby special. Crosby was perfectly suited for Bette: She loved the music of the Andrews Sisters, an act that he had recorded with on many occasions; she was also a dramatic contrast for his laidback style. Yet for Bette, the most important part of the show would be the viewers—Middle America. Bing's shows hit the heartland, and Bette needed to have that heartland love her if she was going to be considered anything more than a crazy fad of an act.

Sadly, Bing died soon after the show was filmed, which meant that the ratings for his last show would be sure to go through the roof. Added to this unusual good fortune was an opportunity to be a featured guest on the *Rolling Stone Tenth Anniversary* special. Viewers who didn't watch Bing would get a chance to see Bette on this show.

Using the success of her first two albums, as well as the television exposure and loads of great reviews for her sold-out concert appearances, Russo and Bette put together a deal with NBC to bring Bette to prime time. The network wanted her act toned down, but beyond that they pretty much left the content of the show up to Bette.

Over the course of the next two months, Bette dropped twenty pounds and added bit of blonde to her hair. Using her own band while adding respectable costars Dustin Hoffman and Emmett Kelly, she tamed her ribald show enough to get into the nation's living room and only offend a very small portion of the viewers.

Old Red Head Is Back was a beautifully conceived special. As a matter of fact, it was so good that it won an Emmy. Bette set the atmosphere for the hour by saying, "Let's shoot the breeze," and in a way, much more than even with her stage show, there was a feeling of real communication between performer and audience.

For the first time, she came across not as a lusty exhibitionist, but as a funny, sincere, loving, warm lady. In the past, when she had presented herself as trash, many felt that she was. Now, the perception was that she was *playing* trash. She never quit being Bette Midler, but there was a Carol Burnett-type aura about her during this show. No longer just a great vocalist and a funny person, she was someone who could really be liked.

This was what she needed. Being known as the "last of the trashy ladies" was not going to propel her to superstardom, nor would it get anyone to take her seriously. On NBC, just a few days short of her thirty-third birthday, Bette Midler began to be seen as a more serious performer.

In retrospect, though, one of her off-the-wall numbers was probably the most memorable: There was Bette, dressed in a bikini, singing "Oklahoma" on a Pacific island set. She then stated that she "was living proof that the moral standards of this country had died," but still came off as being harmlessly sweet. Before then, no one had been quite certain.

The show accomplished for Bette what Broadway and records could not—it made her respectable.

Feeling confident, she opened at the Copacabana in late January and broke all the club's records for attendance. The manager had placed chairs an tables in every possible corner of the room, some without any view of the stage; was charging twenty dollars for a bottle of wine and sixty dollars for champagne; was demanding a twenty-dollar cover charge for each person; and still couldn't keep people out of the club. The normal capacity was 600—for most nights over 1,000 were admitted. With Bette, the Copa was rockin'.

Walking out onto the stage on a rainy opening night, Bette stood up straight, shot her chest out to its fullest position, and proudly announced, "I stand before you nipples to the wind." The crowd died laughing, and the action that followed made everyone there either forget or forgive the outrageous prices, cramped conditions, and heat in the room. Bette was in rare and raw form, proving that television may have toned down her act for America, but she was still the same raunchy mama for the boys back home.

As the night wore on, she said more and more rotten things about the club, sang every number she knew, and finally commented, "You are all fools. They bought Manhattan for less money than it cost you to see me tonight." Later, as the crowd dispersed into the rainy night, Bette and Russo had reason to be pleased. They were working for the live gate, while the club was making its money off the booze sales. Both ended the two-week Copa gig with a lot to smile about.

For those two weeks, the Copa was the place to be if you were a somebody in New York. Mayor Koch not only came to the show, but was the butt of many of Bette's best jokes. Joining him one night was Bess Myerson, and Bette didn't allow Bess to forget that she was Jewish and a former Miss America. Other celebs who attended included Lee Radziwill, Neil Sedaka, Diana Ross, Andy Warhol, Raymond St. Jacques, and Rodney Dangerfield. (Rodney didn't even get a seat until someone became sick and was forced to leave—even at a Midler show he got no respect!)

It was obvious that the fans loved the show, and a few critics did, too. Rex Reed said that it was a "can't-miss" item for early 1978. Others, though, thought it to be a greedy attempt to soak the public, and most noted that Bette's voice was far from solid and that she appeared tired. Still, just as Elvis's weight and inability to remember the words to his biggest hits had never detracted his fans from their worship, so did Bette's fans accept what happened for those few weeks in January. So the show hadn't changed much in a decade. So she hadn't had a hit since Manilow produced her. So her jokes and routines had been reused as much as Milton Berle's. Just being Bette was enough . . . wasn't it?

Even as Bette saw her profits grow into bigger and bigger numbers, she must have realized there had to be more than money. She once again looked to Aaron Russo to find it for her.

7

EVER SINCE COMING TO NEW YORK, THE ALWAYS independent Bette had done one thing that may have seemed out of character. She called home often. Talking to her family and sharing the ups and downs of her career continued to be a very important facet of her life. But now it was even more important.

Bette's mother, Ruth, had been diagnosed as having cancer. It had started in her breasts and spread to her lungs. She was undergoing some very grueling surgery and treatments, and her suffering was tearing Bette up. The distance that separated them had become more and more obvious as her mother's pain grew worse. With her career at an important point, and with the dates she had to play, Bette couldn't get away to see Ruth as much as she wanted, and this was extremely tough, for the two were still so close.

It was also difficult that during this time of stress and fear, Bette's career was in a state of flux. While the Copa and television specials had played well, her subsequent albums were not living up to her earlier successes. *Broken Blossoms* and *Live at Last* caused only ripples in the music world. It was even hard to find reviews of the work. Since Manilow had become a star and was much too busy to help Bette, her best qualities had not again been captured on vinyl.

Many also accused Aaron Russo of mismanaging his star, blaming him for the poor records, the lack of a big tour, no movie deals, and an erratic roadmap for achieving success. It seemed impossible to string major successes back to back. Always between them were unsuccessful records, an unexplained long vacation, rash statements, or an unenthused Bette. Russo needed to pull off a major coup.

One of the first things he did was make a major gaffe. He and Bette announced a worldwide tour (Europe and Australia) and then demanded that they would have to be paid in gold bullion or they wouldn't work. Their reasoning seemed financially logical—the dollar had been taking a beating in foreign markets, and gold would be a way to ensure a profit. The press, as well as many other performers, saw it as a slap in the face of America and began to accuse Bette of being less than patriotic.

Speaking for a host of actors, Robert Stack said, "It could start an unhealthy trend. She represents something super in our profession. If someone [like

Bette] with a high profile does this, then it is a bad precedent. I'd like to think that American performers would be paid in American money."

Many agreed with Stack and questioned if Bette wasn't just a money-hungry woman who cared little for anything other than herself. The bad press on this episode ran for almost as long as the tour did. It certainly didn't help Bette's image or career, and Russo was going to have to pull a big rabbit from his hat to change this perception. Fortunately he did.

Russo's big surprise was the announcement that before Bette left for her tour, she would make her first film. She'd landed a starring role in a project known as *The Rose.*

The movie would only take ten weeks to shoot, but putting it together had taken years. Russo had first been approached about having Bette play the lead in the early 1970s. At that time the project had been given the working title of *The Pearl,* and Marvin Worth at 20th Century Fox was in charge of putting the script by Bill Kerby on film. The script made it more than clear that this was a film about Janis Joplin, even though it claimed to be completely fictional. Bette, who had seen Joplin work on several occasions, didn't like the script, and thought it too soon after the late singer's death to do her story.

Talented director Mark Rydell was given the script in early 1973, and he immediately asked the studio to allow him to pursue Bette as the star. The executives didn't want to have anything to do with Bette at that time, so they took the script from Rydell and handed it to Ken Russell. Five years passed, and somehow the script eventually dropped back into Rydell's hands.

Rydell needed a hit. Early in his career he had scored well with *The Fox, The Reivers, The Cowboys,* and *Cinderella Liberty,* which had been released in 1973 and was his big success. In late 1977, he and screenwriter Bo Goldman began to go through *The Pearl* page by page, revising and rewriting it as less of a story about Joplin and more of a fictionalized account of the downfall of a huge rock star. One of the things they also did was change the title to *The Rose.*

They set the movie in 1969, a time of vast change and inner crisis within the country, wanting an edge to their story that would show the struggle between the ideals of the past and developing social freedoms. They wanted authentic music, euphoric highs, and very deep, depressing lows. It would be a movie like no other, and it would live as close to the edge as the singer upon whose life it was based.

Once again Russo and Bette were approached with the script, and Fox's timing couldn't have been better. Bette needed a film, and Russo needed something to prove to critics that he was responsible for doing things other than confusing his star's career. They jumped at the chance.

Russo joined Marvin Worth as coproducer, but his main job would be to act as a liaison between Bette and the others involved in the project. Bette, in what amounted to an almost one-woman show, would simply be the star. This was something she knew she could do well. Alan Bates and Frederic Forrest had been chosen as her costars.

The shooting began on April 24, 1978 in New York. This was Bette's home, the place where she'd been worshiped for years, and it was little wonder that as the location shots were filmed, thousands of her fans gathered to watch her work. When scenes were completed, the crowds would break out into applause and cheers. It was something the crew had never seen before. They were as amazed as Bette.

The locations included a luxury midtown-Manhattan penthouse, a Lower East Side police station, Brooklyn Heights, the Brooklyn Bridge, a host of city streets, and an office building near Grand Central Station. The shooting there only took two weeks, but it was fourteen days in which Queen Bette held court with her subjects, and the city once again fell in love with the performer.

In Los Angeles things were far different. People didn't seem to care much about the daily shoots or the stars. It was more a business, and this atmosphere reminded everyone, including Bette, just how hard that business of making movies really was. There were long hours, early calls, bad catered food, and tired people with tempers always hanging within seconds of rage. Regardless of all the hard times, there were three special moments, and they were all musical.

Central to the movie's theme was the use of live concerts to echo the authentic feel of the era and the music. The songs written for the movie needed to carry a great deal of the film's passion and energy, so the use of live audiences and real musical set-ups was vital.

The concerts were staged at the Embassy Auditorium, Wiltern Theater, and Long Beach Veterans Memorial Stadium. Months of preparation went into the logistics of filming at these sites, and the shows that resulted were electric.

Musical director Paul Rothchild, a legendary record producer who had worked with Jim Morrison, Janis Joplin, and the Everly Brothers, had put together an eight-piece band made up of some of the best studio and stage musicians in the rock world. Included in this group were Norton Buffalo, Whitey Glan, Danny Weiss, Mark Leonard, Mark Underwood, Robbie Buchanan, Steve Hunter, and Jerry Joumonville. Rothchild had also chosen a dozen hard-hitting, dynamic songs from the over one thousand he had reviewed. Mark Rydell had made him well-aware of the fact that if the music didn't fly, neither would the rest of the film.

The second concert, filmed at the Wiltern, used paying customers as extras. For two exhausting shows, Bette gave a concert made up of the same five songs sung over and over again. The crowd seemed to care little about the repetition; they simply felt that they were seeing a rock performer at her best. When Bette belted out "Midnight In Memphis" and "When a Man Loves a Woman," it always brought them to their feet.

The Long Beach show was also a paid concert, and more than 10,000 rock fans jammed the seats to watch Bette work. Jay Leno was hired to loosen the audience up—and whatever he did worked.

The fans became so caught up in Bette's performance that they began to pull off their clothes, hollering "Sex, drugs, rock'n'roll." Later they chanted "Rose, Rose, Rose" as she closed the show with "Stay With Me."

For Bette, it may have been one of the most powerful moments of her life. For the first time, she was immersed in the driving rhythm of rock music, and its dynamic force and passion helped her beg for the audience's love. The crowd returned it full force, and as the seven cameras caught all the action, it was easy to forget that this was just a movie. It seemed so real; Bette was no longer Bette, but the Rose. If Mark Rydell hadn't known before that this $9 million film was special, he definitely knew now. Yet just a few minutes before this ecstatic moment, he must have been wondering if he had made the right choice.

He and Bette had been involved in a heated argument offstage. Leno had run out of jokes, and it was well past the time for Bette to go on. Saying she was just too tired, she had almost walked. Only Rydell's pleading had kept her there. The crew was wondering if Bette was really tired—or scared. Maybe she didn't think she could become the used-up powerhouse that the script demanded of her.

Then, seconds later, she composed herself and walked out being just as vulgar, as crude, and as dynamic as was called for. She was more than good—she was great.

Of course, music wasn't the whole show and Bette's part was quite difficult. She had to play a great star, heading home and burned out; a drug addict and a user who had been used up. The Rose had problems with her manager, and she never seemed to go anywhere or be capable of doing anything without a bottle of booze in her hand. Unlike the wonderfully trashy ladies that Bette had portrayed in her nightclub acts, the Rose was not someone with very many loving facets.

Englishman Alan Bates played Rose's ambitious manager. This was his first film in Hollywood, despite having been in numerous hits such as *Zorba the Greek, The Fixer, Far From the Madding Crowd, Women in Love,* and *An Unmarried Woman.*

The picture's other lead was Frederic Forrest. The Texas native played the part of Dyer, Rose's boyfriend, who was also an Army deserter. Forrest had grabbed the studio's attention in *When the Legends Die,* and may have been best-known for his portrayal of Lee Harvey Oswald in *Ruby and Oswald.* Others in the cast included Harry Dean Stanton, Michael Greer, Barry Primus, Jack Starrett, and David Keith.

In the behind-the-scenes jobs, Rydell and Fox had assembled a group of professionals who made Bette's transition into movies easier. Oscar-winner Theoni Aldredge was in charge of all costumes; Tony Ray, best-known for is work with *An Unmarried Woman,* was executive producer; and Vilmos Zsigmond, coming off an Oscar for *Close Encounters of the Third Kind,* was the cinematographer.

After the ten-week shoot, Bette decided to hold on to a home in Los Angeles. Packing her bags, she then headed out on her European tour, stopping only long enough to announce a book deal with a major New York publisher. Meanwhile, Rydell, who was thrilled with what he had shot, retired to the cutting room to assemble the hundreds of thousands of feet of film into a movie.

The process would take longer than he planned, though. Original plans were for the film to be released in the spring of 1979. Yet when the previews were held, the audience reaction was not as positive as the studio had hoped. Rydell went back to the cutting room again and again, supposedly lifting some dialogue and adding some music. Still, Fox put the movie on hold. It would be November before they finally worked up enough courage to release *The Rose* and hope it found its market. No one, especially Bette, had been prepared for this eighteen-month wait. But even as bad as Rydell's waiting game must have been, Aaron Russo suffered a worse one.

Russo's often-unexplained actions during the filming of the movie had set Los Angeles on its ear. Bette wanted him to become a more behind-the-scenes mentor, yet he wanted in on every part of her work, to be in the public eye. Often, particularly during *The Rose,* this clash had resulted in shouting matches between the two.

With a film under her belt and with a mound of bad publicity now behind her, Bette was beginning to feel that she could become more involved in her own career choices. When Russo wanted her to return to Broadway—and she wanted to pursue more projects in Hollywood—the rift became more serious. Finally, just a few months after the filming ended, Bette fired her manager of seven years and signed with noted Hollywood agent Arnold Steifed. She also turned over much of the legal nature of her business to attorney Gerry Edelstein. The curtain had been dropped on the man many people had called her Svengali. And for the first time in years, Bette felt free.

8

BEFORE BETTE LEFT FOR EUROPE, SHE SOLD SIMON and Schuster on a book idea. She would write a journal while she was overseas, and then it could be turned into a book containing the same irreverent humor that had made her theatrical shows so popular. The publisher bought the idea and gave her a six-figure advance, yet demanded very little structure concerning the work's content. For a woman who had once considered becoming a librarian, the writing would be a joy—"almost as good as sex."

Bette took some time off, most of it spent coping with her mother's illness and death from cancer. She began to question her own mortality, and this frame of mind found its way into her interviews with the media. She was constantly bringing up the "biological" clock, making remarks about wanting children. Yet at the same time, she was doubting that she could ever find someone she wanted to marry.

Many people felt that despite her ardent social life and often-exhibitionist behavior, deep down inside Bette Midler was really a very proper woman. For years she had masked that part of her through show business, but now, perhaps she was finally ready to grow up.

Bette left on her world tour in early fall, hitting most of Europe, Israel, and Australia. At each stop she was mobbed by her fans and practically canonized by the press. In France they compared her to Groucho Marx and Charlie Chaplin. At every nightspot in the country, a large throng of G.I.s and other expatriates cheered her on. For Bette, who had kept her grief over her mother's death very private, the adulation was thrilling. Bette was back, as strong as ever. In fine voice, she could escape her pain onstage.

Twentieth Century Fox took this opportunity presented by Bette's tour and previewed *The Rose* for foreign audiences. The reviews, though mixed, seemed to give the studio a degree of confidence, and an American release date was slated for November. Just the same, they were less than convinced that Mark Rydell had given them a real hit.

Rydell was talking about the movie everywhere he went, explaining that Bette and the film were very good. He even made light of his "small" disagreements with his female lead, saying, "Bette's talent is unlimited . . . but it is like an open wound. Sometimes you have to toss some salt in it for it to react." The director's words served to pump a degree of curiosity about the project into the Hollywood film community. Still, not all of Rydell's recent work had been that good, and many studio executives wondered if the inexperienced Bette Midler was really suited for film.

Meanwhile, Bette, now a half-a-world away, wrote, planned a return to Broadway, and raked in the dough. In Australia she brought in more than $400,000, and she'd had even larger, more passionate crowds in Europe. Not bad for a one-time act at the Baths.

After returning to the States, Bette played local clubs to polish her upcoming Broadway show. Another one-woman show, this one would show off a trim, well-schooled, and, rumor had it, far less flashy Bette Midler. New Yorkers received an opportunity to see if the rumors were true in September at the Concord Pavilion.

The rumors were partially true. Bette had cleaned up her act a little, but it would still receive an R rating if it were a motion picture. In many ways, with the swing music, the outlandish characterizations, the funny one-liners, and the unique costumes, Bette was still the same old hat. But this show was different in one respect—it seemed to have a message a little deeper than "everything you see and everything that I do is trash." This one seemed to say, "I'm not trash. I'm in control and I'm having fun." This theme would become more obvious when she opened on Broadway in two months.

As Bette reshaped her own show, Fox finally released *The Rose* to mixed reviews. Much like

Bette herself, the movie evoked real passion. People either hated it or they loved it. Some thought it to be nothing more than another rock musical, while others stated that it might be a film that would change the whole course of musical filmmaking. Some thought Bette's character shallow and unsympathetic, but others saw deep undertones of the fabric of our nation in every action.

Time was one of the first national publications to write about *The Rose*. Frank Rick began his review by declaring, "Bette Midler is not a great singer or a subtle actress or an exquisite beauty; yet she just may be a movie star." After giving a blow-by-blow of the best moments of the film, he concluded his review by deciding that the role and the actress were very well-suited for each other. "This is vulgarity at its most absurd and most amusing—and why not? For Bette Midler, self-styled queen of 'trash with a flash,' *The Rose* is an ideal throne."

Jack Kroll, *Newsweek*'s critic, devoted even more space and words to the movie. Unlike other reviewers who saw it as a thinly veiled bio of Janis Joplin, Kroll went so far as to see deep undertones sprinkled throughout the movie. "The stops on the tour became a kind of profane Stations of the Cross; Rose is acting out the passion of a sacrificial deity in the rock culture of the '60s." While Bette herself would question everything that the reviewer read into the film, she would hardly have found fault with his observations concerning her performance. "Bette Midler gives us Rose complete with flower and thorns. It's a fevered, fearless portrait of a tormented, gifted, homely, sexy child-woman who sings her heart out until it exploded. Midler's performance is an event to be experienced."

Many others not only didn't see the symbolism, but failed to lift Bette as high either. Janet Maslin of *The New York Times* admitted that she cared for Bette's performance, but questioned the believability of her part. "Miss Midler herself seems as fragile as a bull elephant, no matter how stridently the screenplay insists that she will eventually self-destruct."

Maybe Archer Winsten of the *New York Post* said it best for hundreds of critics and fans when in his review he saw both sides of the movie. He said that it would "split the public right down the middle. One portion will have to consider it a blazing rendition by Bette Midler of a doomed singer who has some parallels with the late Janis Joplin. The others, no lovers of earsplitting sound, frenzied mass audiences, and characters who indulge heavily in emotion, liquor, drugs, and violence, will rule this picture far out of bounds. There is no middle ground."

Perhaps the best and only way to fully judge the critical merits of the film is in reviews that were done later, after the film and the era it represented could be judged in a manner that had little to do with whether a reviewer felt moved by the subject matter or music. Today, most critics have raised Bette's performance to a status of excellent. There are raves for her power and her singing. The movie itself is rarely rated much above average, due in large part to the heavy-handed script and the movie's predictable ending.

No matter what the critics said about the film, it brought out a large number of fans. The almost $10 million that Fox had invested in the picture was quickly recouped, and the studio could be assured that Rydell and Midler had provided them with a hit. For Bette, this meant the opportunity to look for more work, possibly in a role that would give her a chance to stretch beyond playing an entertainer. It was an important first step in establishing herself as an actress.

Beyond what it could do for her in Hollywood, it also gave her a hit album. The movie audiences had become enthralled with the soundtrack and when the album was released, it went straight to the top of the charts, outselling all of Bette's other albums. In a matter of months it went platinum. *The Rose* had once again legitimized Bette Midler, the singer. For the first time in years, she was hot at the record stores.

"When a Man Loves a Woman" was the first release off the album, and hung in the top forty for three weeks. It ended its reign at a modest thirty-five, but this was Bette's biggest single hit since June of 1973. "The Rose," the second single from the album, stayed in the top forty for sixteen weeks, was certified gold, and became Bette's biggest song of all time when it topped out at number three. It would also be the next-to-last time she would ever have a single in the top forty. But for now, those who knew the recording industry were predicting that this new phase of her career would make her the queen of rock music.

The early success of the movie also helped assure Bette of another big draw on Broadway in her newest vehicle, *Divine Madness.* Arguably, Bette would have probably done very well during her run at the Majestic Theater even if *The Rose* had flopped. After all, the New York crowds had loved her for years, and few of her hard-core fans would judge her on her first movie role. Still, all the press the movie had generated helped to ignite at least a curiosity in a number of non-Midler fans.

When her concert/play/musical opened on December 5, 1979, it was to a different and far more upscale crowd than had caught her *Clams on the Halfshell.* And this was a new show as well. There was more rock music, as well as a more mature Bette. She oozed confidence, and poked fun, told off-color stories, even threatened to flash skin, but she was more controlled.

She opened with a lavish arrangement of "Big Noise From Winnetka," a song dating back to the 1930s but which had a contemporary feel to it via Bette's arrangement. She had dyed her hair almost pink, rather than the blonde of *The Rose,* and wore a very low-cut dress. Her monologues were even more tightly constructed than during her Concord show, and she went so far as to call herself a screen goddess, (and then followed that assessment with the comment, "You know, like Miss Piggy"). Despite her sudden burst of success, she wasn't taking herself too seriously.

Many of the reviews went so far as to call the crowd square, but *reserved* would have been a better word. Jerry Blatt and Bruce Vilanch's writing was appreciated, as was Bette's singing, but it was a different kind of appreciation. This grown-up crowd didn't want to participate—they wanted to be entertained. And so they were. Song after song, for almost two hours, Bette made them laugh a little, smile a lot, and sweat none. A change from the old days, but not necessarily worse—just more mature.

This was no longer the entertainer looking in from the outside. She had money, respect, and position. As the seventies quickly gave way to the more conservative eighties, Bette seemed content not only to accept this new crowd of people who once might have snubbed her vulgarity, but to want to join them.

In interviews she began to talk about growing up and leaving the old, wild days behind. While her act still contained a great deal of raunchiness, she made a point of explaining that in real life, she wasn't that way. She seemed to be taking an eraser and trying to wipe away an image that she had spent a decade creating.

Other acts had managed similar transformations. A generation before, Elvis left for the Army and a nation of older Americans had bid him farewell, hoping that he would be forgotten. Yet he wasn't, and that two-year stint gave him respectability. While he was away, the world changed, and he was no longer viewed as a serious threat to an older generation of entertainers or to the youth of America. He was not only suddenly respectable, he was welcomed back as a sign of the American dream at work.

Bette hadn't left for the Army, and she hadn't

suddenly become a hero. But the country and the times had changed. The common man was now hearing Archie Bunker use taboo words each week on national television. Nixon's famous tapes had been filled with the same kind of language Bette had long used onstage to shock people, and sexual mores loosened as well. All of a sudden, Bette wasn't so bad. And the mere fact that she had weathered and survived potential fadiness meant that there must be something of real substance to her. And everyone was willing to give her a chance.

But Aaron Russo wasn't ready to let the past be forgotten. He stopped by the Majestic, caught Bette's act, and then went backstage to see her. In no uncertain terms he informed her that she was awful. Bette, who at the time was fighting a bad case of the flu, fought back with sharp words of her own. Grabbing a soft drink, Russo poured it over her head and stormed off.

As 1980 rolled in, Bette received a Golden Globe award for her acting in *The Rose*. She was the toast of both Broadway and Hollywood. The Globe was barely cold on her shelf when Bette was nominated for an Academy Award. She didn't win the Oscar, but she did join the select few who had been nominated for their first starring role. When she showed up at the ceremonies, the best of Los Angeles rolled out the red carpet for the newest toast of the town.

Everywhere she would go for the next few months, fans and critics would be shouting, "We love you, Bette!" With every bouquet came a question: "What's next?"

It was a good question. Bette now had so many offers that she really didn't know where to begin looking for the right part or vehicle. All around her people were crying for her to do their movies or their plays. Everywhere she went, people were giving her just the right part or an opportunity for a chance of a lifetime. As an entertainer with over a decade spent building success, Bette had long been approached with offers; however, this time was different. The ones who were making offers weren't dreamers—they were the real, powerful dream-makers. The men and women with whom only the best had a chance to work. And they all wanted Bette.

With the press ready to write about her every move, and with millions of dollars hanging in the balance, Bette was playing with an opportunity to go three different ways. She could return to the studio and see if those who were predicting that she was going to be the female Elvis of the eighties were right. She could grab a handful of movie offers and see if she couldn't take her unique looks and style into an area of film success that few had ever experienced. Or she could return to Broadway, starring in any of a number of big-budget, surefire hits, the kind that would make her the toast of New York and a stage legend forever.

Once, Bette had asked only to be made a legend. Now it seemed that this dream was a foregone conclusion. The only thing that really needed to be decided—how should she choose to make her legendary figure and talents come to life?

NEXT FOR THE DIVINE AND VERY MUCH IN DEMAND Miss M would be the release of a new album, *Thighs and Whispers.* The studio must have decided that the best way to market the new and improved Bette Midler was to take her right down the middle of the road.

Thighs was not as much a recording of Bette Midler music as it was simply good music. Many reviewers complained that they couldn't even find Bette's voice under all the arrangements and strings. This singer who had once surrounded herself with a rough, on-the-edge production had now been wrapped in satin. While her fans, especially the ones who had discovered her via *The Rose,* may have felt misled, most critics liked it.

For the fans, it was just another album. They really didn't care if Bette's voice was in fine form—they wanted to hear her cutting up and having fun. She wasn't someone who entertained them in low lights, over a glass of wine—she was a wild woman whose music wasn't supposed to be romantic, but rather an orgy of excitement, humor, and drive. This was not it.

On the air and in the record stores *Thighs and Whispers* paled in comparison to the soundtrack album for *The Rose.* For a few moments, the ever-present title of legend escaped Bette, yet the lack of sales didn't slow down her desirability in other arenas.

The woman that many were now calling "the phenomenon of the seventies" was approached by a brand-new company looking for a hit to begin its foray into the world of film. By 1980, the most famous Ladd in the world was not the dog or the once-powerful male leading actor, it was a small blonde named Cheryl, who had starred for several years in an ABC-TV show called *Charlie's Angels.*

But the name Ladd would soon reemerge in Hollywood as a force to be reckoned with. Alan's son, Alan Jr. (once Cheryl's husband), was forming a company to produce major features, and he needed a project to kick off this venture. The Ladd Company wanted to capitalize on a star's name and box-office recognition, fast turnaround, and a relatively low budget.

Bette was one of the names often mentioned at The Ladd Company. *The Rose* and her tours had proven that there was an audience for her original act, but finding a vehicle in which she could act while showing off her multiple talents might take years. They needed something much faster than that.

At the time The Ladd Company was setting up shop in Los Angeles, Bette's *Divine Madness* was breaking box-office records on the other coast. The musical was so hot that even West Coast newspapers were sending reviewers to cover it. This coverage, and the energy of the act, didn't escape Ladd's attention. Seeing a chance to take a show that had already been put together, and repackage, reshoot, and ship it out almost overnight to take advantage of the star's Oscar nomination and box-office appeal was just too good to pass up.

Within days of the idea first being discussed, they had Bette's name on a contract, were clearing away time for a Los Angeles shooting, and were assembling a team to bring Broadway to the big screen. The last was the trickiest part. For some reason, the stage didn't convert to the limits of cinema very well. Yet *Divine Madness* was really as much a concert and club show as it was a play.

Of course, there were also drawbacks. For starters, would Americans pay four bucks to see a film of a concert show when they had recently (by industry standards) seen Bette for free on NBC? Concerts also seem to play much better in person than onscreen. (Twice the cameras had tried to catch the magic of Elvis on film, and on both occasions the energy just wasn't there.) Still, the low cost of writing and production overruled the Ladd organization's other doubts.

William Fraker, the famed cinematographer, joined executive producer Howard Jeffrey and producer/director Michael Ritchie on the project. Backing them up were choreographer Maria Blakely, and Bette's two friends and longtime writers, Bruce Vilanch and Jerry Blatt. Adding an experienced camera and sound crew, coupled with the normal stable of technical people, the team was completed.

The rest of the cast consisted of people that had worked on Broadway with Bette. Jocelyn Brown, Ula Hedwig, and Diva Gray made up the Harlettes, now very famous for their immoral support. Bette's regular boys—Randy Kerber on keyboards; Joey Carbone and Dave Shank on percussion; Tony Berg on guitar; drummer Art Wood; bassist John Pierce; and sidemen Chas Sanford, Dave Luell, Rich Copper, and Jon Bonnie—made up her band.

Ladd would tell the press that his aim was to "break down the barrier between the screen and the audience. To capture the energy . . . and spontaneity of a live performance." His first move in doing this, after assembling his crew, was booking the Pasadena Civic Auditorium for three nights. The art deco showplace sold out almost as soon as the shows were announced, as the afficionados of the "Queen of Flash and Trash," a title that Bette was beginning to outgrow, descended on the box office.

Producer Ritchie had seen enough of Bette Midler to know that her fans were as much of a show as she was. He didn't want, nor could he let, his cameras and filming get in the way of this important element of the show. If his people slowed down or stopped the performance's energy, then what was unique and special about a Bette Midler show would be lost. In lecturing his crew he pointed out the need for them to blend in, not to get in the way, to almost not even be noticed or felt. He told them, "They [the fans] know her lyrics by heart. They mimic her gestures. They throw straight lines and she hurls back jokes like firecrackers. We can't miss that."

Ritchie stationed not three or even four, but *ten* cameras around the auditorium in order to capture every moment of the star and her fans. The ultra-sophisticated sound system was complemented by a battery of 1,600 lights. Nonetheless, as much instrumentation and technical equipment as there was, everything remained almost invisible. When the actual movie was completed, not one camera was ever shown. The theater audience never saw the filming process and had a better chance to become involved, much as they would if they had attended the show in person.

This subtle camera technique made the film work. Ritchie captured the real Bette and her real fans because he took care to catch every moment of every night from every possible angle. Putting it together proved a special kind of hell, but the end result was as close to a live event as had ever been filmed. That, to most Midler fans, was pure heaven.

Glenn Farr was the man who whittled down the ninety hours of film into a two-hour movie. For several months, all he did was live and relive the shows. It was a wonder he didn't overdose on Bette, and he must have been glad when he was finished cutting. So were a lot of other people. They bought tickets in bunches.

The Ladd Company had a hit; the reviews were sometimes wonderful, and rarely bad. In the *Bos-*

ton Phoenix, Alan Stern compared Bette to three contemporaries and made her the winner. "Unlike Liza Minnelli, Midler has a presence that hints at a real person lurking behind the razzle-dazzle; unlike Streisand, she connects with and draws energy from a live audience; unlike Miss Piggy, she's the joke and she knows it." His favorite line from the film: "Once you reach thirty, your body decides it wants a life of its own."

Variety called it a worthy followup to her first starring role. In a three-star review, Ernest Leogrande in the New York *Daily News* summed up the film by writing, "The seemingly inexhaustible Midler ends her screen performance by standing on her head, a fitting symbol of the lengths she goes to in order to deliver the show she feels is expected of her."

Leogrande's statement may have been the biggest and best commentary of what The Ladd Company was able to accomplish. They brought Bette's energy alive on film. The result was that Bette Midler was now appreciated by millions of people who had never had the chance to understand just why her live performances were so special.

The movie, as well as the energy it revealed, was important. *Thighs and Whispers* had contained little momentum, and what was there seemed forced. *Divine Madness* showed and projected the energy that made the star unique, almost a legend. For those critics who wondered if the real Bette and her style had been used up, this proved that she was still growing as an entertainer.

A second point was also proved by the movie.

Bette's humor, now toned down even more than the year before, was beginning to reach a point where it could be accepted by mainstream audiences and still be funny. Along with Richard Pryor, she had used vulgarity to draw laughs. While raunchiness was still a part of her act, it was not so prominent. She was discovering that she could be funny without cussing, and that she could turn heads and command attention without dropping her top. These were all signs of large gains in self-esteem and maturity.

In May of 1980, Bette added another chapter to her life when Simon and Schuster released her book, *A View From a Broad.* Scores of critics rushed to review the book, and *After Dark* even laid down big bucks to run excerpts of it. The manuscript proved to be as unique and wordy as the writer.

For starters, no one could have walked by and not noticed it. It made every other book sharing shelf space with it look, well, bland and unexciting. The cover was a rainbow of bright, blazing color, and in the middle of this rainbow was a photo of Bette. This wasn't just any photo. The lady was shown with her bare arms outstretched toward the sun, her face turned toward the side in a shy, almost withdrawn sort of manner, her eyes closed, but a huge smile shaping her face into a vision of mystical mischief. The other obviously noticeable things were the two small, gold-sequined starfish covering Bette's huge and well-publicized, as she would say, "knockers."

Bette gave Simon & Schuster a small book, barely bigger than a standard paperback, but one with a big return. It was crammed with photos, almost all done in a unique, technicolor style, and descriptive writing filled with off-the-wall observations. Those who bought it swore that it was a "good read."

No other book on the market showed its writer dressed like a giant hot dog. Few travel books of the period presented the art of hugging a kangaroo. And the photos continued to be worth laugh after laugh, no matter how many times fans looked through the book. But the writing made it something really special.

"There's good humor, and many solid guffaws, in Bette's multitude of bawdy stories . . . think of this book as a hot diary; a new-wave yearbook; a collection of Halloween-type drag snapshots," said Douglas Cramer, better-known from being half of the Spelling and Cramer team that created numerous hit shows and movies for ABC-TV. Why was he reviewing the book? Only *The Hollywood Reporter* knows for sure—but he liked it a lot. And so did a number of professional critics.

Why the book worked, and why it went into multiple printings as soon as it was released, was probably due to the fact that it was what the readers expected from Bette . . . something fabulous, and something like they had never read before. Just like her concerts and Broadway shows, it was a one-of-a-kind, brightly colored package filled with slightly naughty stories and lots of things readers probably wished they had said first.

No one but Bette could take a fantasy tourist on a trip like this one. From Seattle to London, all over Europe, then to Australia, Honolulu, and back to Los Angeles, this junket was unique and every word proved it. Still, behind her dedication page—"To Frank Lloyd and Wilbur Wright, without whom this book would not have been possible"—behind the overviews of lumberjacks and the Queen of England, and just preceding those pages poking fun at the Aussie's macho image, were a few pages that actually screamed for something other than a laugh to jump out.

In Germany, the Jewish Bette had begun to feel claustrophobic. There, she viewed the ruins of concentration camps and heard the horror stories of Hitler's insane war machine in action. Humor seemed nonexistent for a moment, and Bette, with her tiny, manual Remington, seemed to be writing between the lines, crying out for the millions whose cries had gone unheard. As she told *The New York Times,* "Do I really believe that bygones should be bygones? It was a very dismal experience."

Bette's book asked us to laugh at the world, making fun of different countries' traditions, history, culture, and people. And it presented a person who blatantly asked not to be taken seriously—and yet, for a brief moment, a compassion and depth came out that even the secretive singer couldn't mask. Bette Midler could hurt for someone and something other than herself.

Except for that one passage, *A View From a Broad* was not meant to allow the reader to get inside Bette's mind or soul; she presented herself as a caricature of a real person. But from press interviews, it was obvious that a real person was inside wanting to break out—and perhaps even escape the world's view of the Divine Miss M.

She told Diane Robbins of the New York *Daily News,* "I once said that I wanted to be a legend and it's been reprinted a million times. I guess everyone thought I had lot of nerve. Well, what I really meant is that I don't want to be anonymous." In the same interview Bette went on to admit that she didn't want to die and not have anyone notice.

Deep down, Bette, the woman who had conquered the movies her first time out, had earned a Grammy and a certain amount of success in the record business, and the entertainer who owned Broadway each time she stepped onstage, still seemed to lack a degree of self-confidence. Now that everyone knew who Bette was—did she know herself?

10

BETTE SHOULD HAVE BEEN RIDING HIGH, YET THERE seemed to be a restlessness in her soul. Something was missing in her life. Part of that something could have been a man. Bette had split up with her latest boyfriend and wasn't content to settle in with just another guy. She wanted more. Even though she had denied over and over again that she ever wanted to get married, she often spoke of her desire to have children. For someone who lusted after immortality, the act of motherhood might be the one way to assure herself of some kind of lasting legacy.

Even if Bette had some doubts, those around her assured her that everything was wonderful. Her book was making money and creating a great deal of praise as a new outlet for her talents. Her movie career seemed assured, and offers were pouring in for all kinds of different roles for top directors at the most powerful studios. Even though her latest album hadn't created huge sales, the reviews were not bad, and the soundtrack to *The Rose* had once again assured her an important spot in the recording world. And bookers, those responsible for concerts and tours in every corner of the globe, wanted her to take tons of money (even paid in gold bullion if she desired) in order to bring her special show to their cities.

Any bright person would have bet that Bette was in a no-lose situation. She may have been living in Los Angeles, but her career was residing high in the clouds. She was not only a star, but one of the brightest.

At the 1982 Academy Awards presentation, Bette was the hit of the evening and literally stole the show. Wearing a bright dress that showed off her two biggest charms, she whisked in to present the award for Best Song, and then cut every one of the tunes to pieces before announcing the winner. Those in attendance, as well as the audience at home, were falling out of their chairs. The longer she raved, the more they laughed. Beyond a shadow of a doubt, it was the high point of the telecast. Once she had owned the Baths—now she owned the world.

From an ego standpoint, it had to be a wonderful experience to be told that you had "made it" by some of the greatest names in the business. Bette was now being applauded for just showing up at a gala. Everyone was assuring her that she was a box-office draw, that she had super talents, and that she was going to continue to ride this wave for years to come. No one or nothing could stop her now.

After a while, any person in Bette's position would probably begin to believe all this great hype. And why not? The bank accounts were bulging, and she was the prime invite on every social mogul's party guest list. People would laugh when she said anything, funny or not. Few people did, or even dared, say no to her anymore. She was one of the world's beautiful people.

Yet underneath it all was a woman bright enough to realize that many people had gotten to the can't-miss point in their lives and then struck out. Bette didn't have the self-confidence to believe that life from now on would be easy.

Not wanting to tour for a long while, she began to sift through the mounds of scripts that had been sent her way. She wanted something that would show the fun range of her acting talents, and something that would be funny and spirited. After weighing many possibilities, one part stood out.

Jinxed promised to be a film that would work well. It was a black comedy at a time when the public seemed ready for this type of humor. It was directed by Don Siegel, a man whose reputation for making successful movies was well-known. And besides Bette (who had been given a great deal of control over the path of the project), it would star a talented veteran, Rip Torn, and heralded newcomer, Ken Wahl. With the screenplay by Bert Blessing and David Newman, this movie should have been a sure thing.

Siegel should have found working with Midler

and Wahl an interesting and challenging job . . . nothing he couldn't handle. He had a history of taking people whose egos were burning as hot as their fame and channeling their energies into good film work. More important, he had gotten brilliant performances out of some actors who were far from the best. In 1956 he took B-actors Dana Wynter and Kevin McCarthy and a throwaway idea and made *Invasion of the Body Snatchers,* now regarded as one of the best science-fiction pieces of all time. There is little doubt that he was largely responsible for paving a new road for Clint Eastwood through his production and direction of *Dirty Harry.* He directed John Wayne in the Duke's best late-career role, that of the dying gunfighter in *The Shootist.* And back in 1960, Siegel had performed what many in Hollywood still consider a miracle. He uncovered a great deal of talent in a well-known entertainer whose film career had been largely considered a joke up until that time—Elvis Presley. Using Presley in a nonsinging role, Siegel honed the entertainer's talents in a Western with heavy racial overtones. The result, *Flaming Star,* was the best of Presley's thirty-three films.

With this wealth of experience behind him, the director felt confident that he would work magic with his current stars. Little did he realize that *Jinxed* would be jinxed from day one.

The premise of the film was fairly simple. Wahl was a blackjack dealer named Willie, who fell madly in love with Bette's character, Bonita. Bonita simply wanted to get rid of her benefactor, Harold, played by Rip Torn, a man whom she served as mistress. Willie and Bonita planned to kill Harold for his life insurance, which paid out to Bonita. The rest of the plot concerns the two lovers' attempts at killing Harold, then Harold's suicide, and then the attempts by the two to prove that they didn't commit the crime. It was supposed to be a funny *The Postman Always Rings Twice.* Could a film be funny, suspenseful, and passionate at the same time? At least *Jinxed* provoked high and uncontrolled passion.

No one knows who began the war that raged during the entire filming. Bette would blame Ken Wahl, and certainly he had his role in the conflict. And the war wouldn't end until months after the picture was released.

Wahl was twenty-four and hot. He was also cocky. Supposedly his first words to Bette were, "I hate niggers and faggots," the latter supposedly being a reference to her large gay following. Certainly this was not a good introduction to someone who was as open-minded as Bette. Still, all the critics had predicted that he would be a superstar, and Wahl didn't care. After all, one didn't have to be a nice guy to be able to act.

Wahl's high talent assessment was based on two films. The first was *Fort Apache, The Bronx,* an inner-city cop film that starred Paul Newman. The next was *The Soldier,* a spy thriller in which all the other actors supported him. Chicago-born and more than a bit rebellious, Wahl's vision of the world couldn't have been more different than Bette's.

Wahl, who only two years before had been pumping gas for a living, didn't really care if people recognized his talent or his charm. All he said he wanted out of the business was money. He hadn't bothered to have his teeth straightened or capped. He wore clothes that were often purchased from surplus stores, did few interviews, and as almost a defiant statement of "nothing is going to change me" drove a 1968 Dodge. He was not a regular on anyone's social list and didn't want to be. He was blue collar all the way. He refused to move to Hollywood, keeping his digs in Chicago. He had no patience for anyone who thought they were better than someone else simply because of their status. Most of all, he didn't want to work with people who thought of themselves as *stars*.

He'd had no problems with Newman. Paul drove race cars and was rarely seen at the Hollywood social gigs. In his other film, the actors had mostly been foreign and were not caught up in being famous or going Hollywood. But with Bette, a woman whose music and looks went unappreciated before the filming, his rebellious side immediately exposed itself.

As he told a large number of different interviewers after the film had been shot, "[Bette] had director approval and cast approval. She abused that power. Even if she had good ideas, she went about it in the wrong way." He determined that Bette wasn't going to steamroll him.

From day one the two of them fought. Attempting to keep the peace were Siegel and Rip Torn. Torn, a Texas actor who had first jumped into public view two decades before in *Baby Doll*, knew that hostility on the set could ruin a good film.

Ultimately, he was probably glad that he was killed off long before the shooting ended. Supporting actors Jack Elam and Benson Fong were not so lucky. World War III, as many gossip columnists called it, waged on and they were usually hit in the crossfire.

Filming was often delayed as Bette stormed off the set, crying and cussing. Gossip columnist Liz Smith and others began to report on the battles with blow-by-blow descriptions of each new flareup. Because Wahl talked to the press, his side was most often revealed. So, day after day it went on, with Wahl becoming more surly and Bette more nervous. By the end of the shooting, she felt as isolated as she had as a child.

Wahl, after having experienced Bette's wrath for weeks, kept talking about the "hell" he had just been through. He told Liz Smith that the only way he could kiss Bette was to pretend that she was something pretty and lovable, like his dog. (Bette countered with wondering if he always made love to his dog.) He went on in other interviews to say that love scenes with the singer were as gross as anything he had ever done. Even after Bette's attorney visited him, issuing a strong warning about slanderous remarks, Wahl continued to talk. He wanted the world to know just what he had been through and just how much of a bitch his costar really was.

Bette was hardly remaining silent. She didn't have any nice things to say about Wahl, and she further claimed that director Siegel had hit her in the jaw. She called the crew and the film the most rotten situation that she had ever been through, and that it had almost killed her. While it was true that the crew may have grown to dislike her, Siegel grew to hate her.

To those around him, it looked as if the director had lost control of his movie, that Bette had the final say on everything. By the midpoint of the shoot, he was finding it as difficult to stomach the ego problems as was Wahl. When the film finally wrapped, Siegel went public, declaring that he would never work with Bette Midler again. Wahl quickly seconded the motion. For her part, Bette didn't want to work with Siegel or Wahl either.

While the remainder of the cast and crew kept quiet about who was to blame, the press and the film world seemed to get the message through the grapevine that Bette had been the biggest villain. Popular opinions of the time labeled her as spoiled, conceited, and impossible in any working situation. Suddenly, almost overnight, she was wearing an invisible label that warned everyone in the film community that she was "unemployable."

What had gone wrong? A number of theories circulated among her friends and associates. One was that she simply thought she was such a big star that the world should play by her rules. This one lined up with the industry view of Bette as a spoiled brat. Certainly Aaron Russo could have testified to seeing some of this behavior in her past.

Another theory was that she felt Torn and Wahl were not high-enough-caliber stars to be sharing her bill, and because of this, they should have been glad to do things her way and not argue for compromises. Wahl and others thought that she had placed herself on this higher level, and the way the gossip columns reported it, the newspaper reader could have easily seen it this way, too.

Had Bette been reading too much of her own publicity?

Perhaps, but a more likely reason for her outbursts might be found in the pressure that she felt before and during the filming. For two years she had traveled the world, almost constantly working. She had pushed herself in film, onstage, and via a book—and done it all with very little help. Aaron Russo was gone, and she was handling most of her own decisions. She had been buried with all the details that she didn't even realize were a part of the business side of her career. The pressure of making the correct choices, hiring and firing people, or setting up and making the final decisions was increased because she knew that if she failed, she would have no one to blame but herself.

On top of all that, there was a lack of personal satisfaction that Bette seemed to exhibit in all of her interviews. She wanted more out of life. Not more awards, not more money, not more fame—but something else. She often said it was children. More likely it was love and acceptance.

Bette had no one guiding her, no Manilow for her music and no Russo for her performances. There was no one waiting to hold her and love her at home. And lonely people are often hostile people, striking out in an effort to reach out. In many ways, Bette may have been in this posture throughout the filming of *Jinxed*.

Whatever it was that made her act the way she did, it all but killed her in Hollywood. Less than a year after she had been heralded as a sure thing, she was at the bottom again, being called a has-been. While Wahl was working, her phone was silent. In a matter of weeks, she retreated, and then collapsed.

For the next six months, Bette spent almost all of her time in bed. She had lost it, and she would later admit on a *Barbara Walters Special* that it was almost more than she could handle. She spoke of the abuse she had given out on the set, and how she still didn't know why she had done it. She also revealed the depths of her depression. "I thought a couple of times I was going to go under. I was ready to call the men in the white suits."

For a half-year, a time when her movie was in postproduction and her career was on a free dive to the pits, she isolated herself from the real world as well as from all of her characters and creations. Her bed, her books, and her pain surrounded her—and engulfed her.

During much of the time she spent in bed she cried for hours without knowing the reason. She saw a psychiatrist, yet nothing and no one seemed to help. Some who'd known her well began to wonder if this woman, a friend who had always lived on the edge, was now *over* that edge. Others scanned the papers looking for a death-by-suicide obituary.

Like so many before her, Bette was now tormented by her own dreams and ambitions. Success hadn't made her happy, and failure had brought her to the lowest point in her life. During her highs the world had been at her beck and call. Now she was miserably alone.

Ironically, even as she lay abed, the reviews (which surfaced) of *Jinxed* were not that bad. Some critics, like devoted Midler fan Rex Reed, had panned it, saying, "It is living proof that shaking your fanny is no longer enough." But most at least thought it was average. The public, however, didn't buy it.

In that fickle world of stardom, Bette was thought to be a star that had shown brightly for a few moments and then burned out.

Aaron Russo and Bette Midler were a romantic item for almost six months. The former rock concert producer was banned from the bedroom but remained in the front office as Bette's manager for seven more years. This photo (taken at a "Friars" roast of Johnny Carson) shows them in the early stages of their relationship.

The premier of *Footloose* offered Bette an opportunity to show off her then-boyfriend Benoit Gautier. Friends said that he showed little compassion when Bette suffered her breakdown soon after completing *Jinxed*. Not long after that they parted.

Bette and the Harlettes, her longtime backup group, in a bit from the hit Broadway musical, *Clams on the Halfshell Revue*. The Harlettes once boasted Melissa Manchester as a part of the trio. Bette often jokingly played up these talented vocalists as the cheapest sluts in New York.
© BOB SCOTT/ NEAL PETERS

Bette Midler and Shelley Long proved to be a female odd couple in the movie *Outrageous Fortune*. Everyone knew that Disney was expecting the two to give them a hit, but few knew that Bette was expecting something, too. Within months of the wrap, Disney had a hit and Bette had a baby girl!
© PHOTOTEQUE

In a rare "Fabian" shot, Bette is shown in a dazzling closeup. The star rarely pushed the glamour angle even in her publicity stills, usually showing more staged, off-the-wall looks. The real Bette does look much more like this photo.

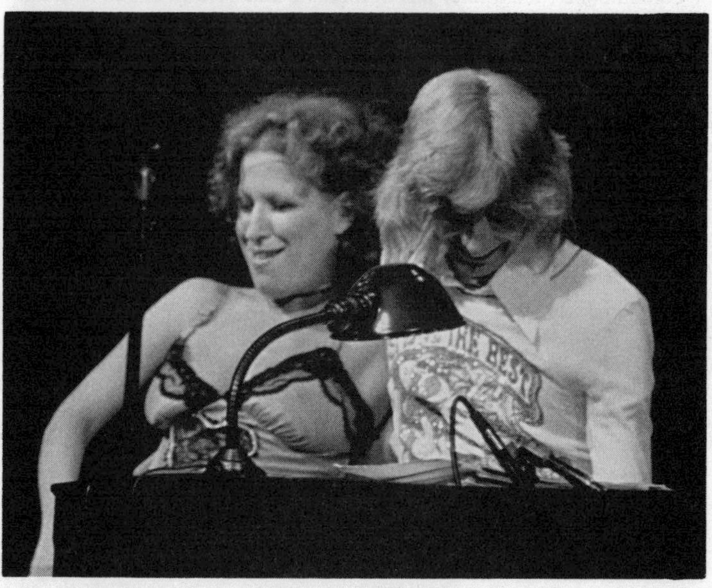

A dynamite combination of Bette and Barry Manilow first wowed the gays at New York's Continental Baths in the early 1970s. The two didn't hit it off at their initial meeting, but this team proved so successful that Barry produced not only two years' worth of live shows, but Bette's first two albums. One of them won a Grammy.

Lily Tomlin jumped into the national scene in the 1960s when her unique humor charmed audiences on NBC's *Laugh In*. Lily's idol was the woman who reigned over the airwaves in the 1950s, Lucille Ball. Bette, the female comedy hit of this decade, linked the two comediennes at a dinner just before she and Tomlin began filming *Big Business* for Disney. © GREG DE GUIRE/CELEBRITY PHOTO

Just after *Down and Out in Beverly Hills* had revived Bette's career, she and new hubby Martin von Haselberg attended the opening night of Mikhail Baryshnikov's performance with the American Ballet Theater. © RON GALELLA

Bette had been a mother for only three months when she and husband, Martin von Haselberg—*aka* Harry Kipper—attended the Moving Picture Ball of the American Cinematheque at the Hollywood Palladium. © SMEAL/GALELLA LTD

Throughout the late 1970s and 1980s, Bette graced the stage with countless high-energy performances. With her quick wit, dynamic voice, and fantastically outrageous costumes, Bette always gave the fans their money's worth. © EBET ROBERTS

Few stars have ever been nominated for an Oscar for their first performance—but Bette was. *The Rose* offered her a chance to shine in a role that seemed tailor-made for her style, and the movie would turn out to be one of the biggest films of the late 1970s. The soundtrack would also bring Bette her first single in years and her first platinum recording ever. © PHOTOTEQUE

Bette Midler once thought about being a librarian. Thankfully she took to the stage instead, but she has written two books to prove that she still has a warm place for literature. *A View From a Broad* came first, then her children's epic, *The Saga of Baby Divine*. A new book on motherhood is due out soon. © DE GUIRE/GALELLA LTD

Bette once said that all she really wanted was to be a legend. Perhaps Hollywood took a large step in recognizing Bette's dream when they gave her her own star. A little-known fact is that she is one of the few women to have won an Emmy, a Tony, and a Grammy. Can Oscar be far behind?

© JOHN PASCHAL/ CELEBRITY PHOTO

This publicity still taken from *Divine Madness* is a typical Bette photo release — showing the joker who for years has charmed the hearts and won the eternal approval of her fans. Bette has a unique look, but no one had really defined it. Perhaps she came closest when she called herself "The Last of the Trashy Ladies."

© PHOTOTEQUE

11

"YOU KNOW WHAT IS SAD?" BETTE HAD SAID WHILE IN the middle of her bluest period. "There is no such thing as the kind of happiness that sticks around. And nobody tells you that's the normal human condition. But I try not to let it worry me. I don't sit around thinking, 'What's wrong with me? Why aren't I happy?' Because now I know the only thing wrong is that I was born a homo sapien."

A new Bette, one attempting to make a statement about not only her own fall and unhappiness, but the world's in general, emerged from her bedroom. After more than six months of exile, she began to attempt to rebuild her career. It was time to rise from the ashes. Either that or die.

For Bette, the one area where she still had some degree of self-confidence was onstage. Grabbing her best old routines, adding new ones, and putting together a band, she began rehearsals for a cross-country tour. It would be called *De Tour,* and as she warbled and danced her brains out for the first three months of 1983, many people wondered if it wouldn't be a farewell tour. After all, how much longer could the "Queen of Camp" carry on?

For Bette, being the Queen was becoming a more and more lonely experience. Now after the shows, she would go to her hotel room and read, wondering why her relationships with men rarely lasted more than a few months and why her heart seemed so heavy. For others it seemed obvious as to why she hurt so—she was a queen without a king.

During her long days on tour, she would put on her thick glasses, take off all of her makeup, dress in some kind of nondescript clothes, and wander the city streets, touring the shops in the locations she was playing. No one would ever have recognized the brown-haired singer. She looked far more like a middle-aged Jewish matron than an entertainer who nightly transformed herself into a talented but slightly raving lunatic. In public she was calm—almost shy and demure.

In interviews, when she was asked about the pilgrimages, she would always joke that she was looking for a good pan. In reality, she was probably looking for peace, hope, and making some meaning out of the jumble that was human life. It was doubtful that the streets of San Francisco, or Chicago, or Detroit could offer her the insight she needed. But still she looked.

Meanwhile, during the evening in backstage dressing rooms, she would make herself once again into a character who'd made her famous. It was her entertainment alter ego, still proudly strutting her stuff to tunes like "I Will Survive." The way she talked offstage, however, led to questions if the real Bette would.

She told the *San Francisco Chronicle* that television was to blame for much of her generation's unhappiness. "Television dehumanizes us. I think that my generation is the last generation of human beings. They [the people growing up now] are different. They lack a conscience. And they lack real heart. It's already shown up. Children today kill with no conscience."

For those that had interviewed Bette on other tours, words like this pointed out that she was far different from the old partying Divine Miss M. Sure, onstage she was still trashy, but off the hardwood she seemed to be a philosopher looking for reason among the inane masses—and finding none.

Even when pressed to speak about her bitter experience during the filming of *Jinxed,* Bette appeared distant and dispassionate. Her words about her costar and director were no longer biting or caustic, and she even seemed to admit that she may have been at least a bit at fault in the matter. The one thing that she didn't do was fight with either her words or her actions. It was over, and she was dealing with it simply as a bad experience that had allowed her to grow up and look at the world a great deal more realistically. This was certainly not the reaction gossip columnists hoped for.

The one thing Bette did talk about was making more movies—funny ones, this time. She wanted to make people laugh. She felt that if given the chance, she would have audiences rolling in the aisles. She also admitted that no one really wanted to deal with her, and her chances of doing a movie again were very slim.

The tour, though not the newsmaking event of her other major showcases, still received good reviews (which Bette refused to read), and great crowds. But as it went on, Bette seemed to be growing more and more tired. She was still attempting to climb onstage and give them all she had, but each night the fuel driving her seemed to contain less energy. Finally, in Detroit, she collapsed during a performance.

She had been sick before the show, vomiting and complaining of a bad headache. In the middle of "Pretty Legs and Big Knockers," she fell down while reaching for a breast-shaped balloon that made even her boobs look tiny, and those onstage knew that she was in trouble. When the balloon appeared onstage without the star, the audience must have figured that something was going on, too. Quickly the curtain fell, and within minutes a voice asked for a doctor.

Many wondered if this wasn't the end, much like Bette's character in *The Rose*. Bette was rushed panic-stricken to the hospital. She wanted to see her mother, a woman who had been dead for almost four years. She thought about all of her friends, and she mourned the fact that she would never see any of them again. What a way for a woman to go, alone in a strange city surrounded by medical professionals who didn't know her from any other Jane Doe. This wasn't the way she had planned it—not at all.

Those at the hospital knew that she was getting better, however, when she began to joke that the only reason she didn't die was to keep the IRS from taking all of the $8 million she was pulling in from *De Tour*. As her temperature came down from a high of 104 degrees, those around her quit worrying, too. The doctors decided she had collapsed from a combination of heat, exhaustion, and a gastrointestinal ailment. All things considered, they deemed her lucky to have let it go so long and not have suffered a worse fate. She healed so quickly that within days she was back onstage.

Probably the biggest stop on Bette's long tour was Radio City Music Hall. Here, the New Yorkers who'd always loved her welcomed her home in style. A lot of the old faces were back, but so were many new ones. Those in the know estimated that gays made up only 10 percent of the crowd. Bette was still a hit with the mainstream masses. And her fans didn't know or care who Don Siegel and Ken Wahl were. They just wanted to see the lady they knew as Divine. Unlike at the beginning of the tour, Bette seemed ready to have a little faith in mankind and be willing to fight a bit for herself.

The first group of people she lashed out at were located on the West Coast. "I cry every night—I do," she told Arthur Bell of the *Village Voice*. "I shed the odd tear for the demise of the studio system . . . I thought I would make movies and get some help from the moguls. Nobody gives you help. They're too busy covering their own asses."

She then began to pick on every one associated with *Divine Madness,* a movie that she had been fairly positive about until now. Gaining momentum, she jumped on the cast of *Jinxed.* Before she was through, very few people she'd ever met in Los Angeles had escaped her sword. Suddenly fiesty, combative, hungry, she appeared ready to take on anyone and anything to once more claim her legendary status. Hollywood could shove it; her tour proved that she didn't need them. But she wanted them to know that she thought *they* needed *her.*

The movie business had sold her short, she said. She painted herself as the innocent, taken in by the wolves whose only desire was to exploit her and then throw her away. And much like a politician running from scandal, she would imply over and over again that her fans still loved her. Still, because she was talking, most of the press and her friends knew that in her heart, it *did* matter what the powers in Hollywood thought; Bette wanted a movie career as badly as she ever wanted anything. If not, why would she have bought a house in the middle of the film establishment?

The house where Bette often retreated seemed very much unlike the public persona of the star. Mediterranean in style and perched on a slope in Coldwater Canyon, it was dark, and many of the rooms were all but empty. Built in 1927, it had hosted many parties and seen many stars enter its doors; Mary Pickford, another misunderstood star, had once called it home.

Bette was nearly forty. She had just ended a three-year off-and-on relationship with a French publicist, Benoit Gautier. She had never claimed he was the love of her life, but it was still hard to be single again, especially for a woman who craved love and a family. Where was a man strong enough to challenge her, flexible enough to allow her to be herself, and trustworthy enough to know her heart?

When not touring, Bette spent time thumbing through a rhyming dictionary, trying to find words she could use to make up a children's book. She had long been fascinated by the way little kids thought, and after discussing both her fascination with children and her love of Disney-style artwork with illustrator Todd Schorr, she touched base with Crown Books and hit them with the idea of a Bette Midler fairy tale/parable/epic poem about a little girl who resembled an infant Bette. An enthusiastic Crown bought the idea for $50,000 and wanted it rushed out. In a way, Bette saw it as a chance to make people a little more human, and as it turned out, her project, much like Disney imagery, could be enjoyed by all ages.

Much more than her first book, *The Saga of Baby Divine* revealed a part of the fabric of the real Bette Midler's heart. Here was a story of hope, a book spreading the belief that people should overcome fear and stand on their own. This was the recent story of Bette's own life, and she had overcome the fear of failure to stand on her own and rise to the top again. But, just like Bette, the book was more than this, too.

Baby Divine could best be described as a Kewpie-doll baby, outfitted in purple high heels and feather boa. Her favorite word was "More!" And the little child desired a life lived as a legend. At the same time, however, Baby Divine was speaking to an entire generation that embraced the idea that money and fame would buy happiness.

The book was about "The Truth," a truth that Bette had only recently discovered. The glamour of carrying thirty-five people from city to city for six months at a time had worn off. Sweating onstage to thrill a few thousand people and read your name in lights didn't seem very grand either. As a matter of fact, having everyone know who you were and watch your every success and failure didn't seem to contain much satisfaction at all. In Bette's own life, she had been happier, without then realizing it, when performing at the Baths and living in a cheap hotel than she had been while making a big-budget motion picture and living like a goddess.

As the book sold well, Bette did a sixteen-city tour to promote it. HBO then announced that it would be showing a new Bette Midler music special in August. Unfortunately, though, *Art or Bust* had been filmed during some of her worst nights of *De Tour,* and it was not Bette at her best. It had slick costumes, wonderful humor, and bright choreography, but not the sharp, full Midler voice; she sounded hoarse. Even her bit as Delores Del Lago, the old lounge singer (part of her act for a decade) outfitted as a mermaid and spinning across the stage in a motorized wheelchair, didn't save the show.

Fred Rothenberg, reviewing the special for the Associated Press, had a suggestion that probably upset Midler but summed up what most critics seemed to think. His backhanded compliments concluded this way: "*Art or Bust* makes for fine viewing. Maybe audiences should watch Miss Midler's eccentric antics with the volume turned down."

Yet the most important point as 1982 turned into 1983 was that Bette's voice volume was down, period. No longer did she have to scream in order to get people to pay attention to her. She was dressing down in public, talking and writing about things other than herself, and was no longer sold on doing anything to excess. She had toned herself down.

She also seemed to be reconciled with the fact that she couldn't have everything, that everyone wasn't going to love her, that all the reviews weren't going to be good, and that she wasn't going to have a man to marry and a baby to carry. She would accept it and go on.

The past twelve months had proved something not only to America but to Bette herself. Unlike many others who had reached out and become legends for a while, she wasn't going to let it kill her. Bette Midler had come quietly back, and now she knew she could survive.

12

AS 1983 PASSED INTO 1984, BETTE, STILL FEELING the strain of doing a book and a tour, simply wasn't seen much. Despite the money her tour had made, despite the success of her saga of Baby Divine, she kept a low profile.

As the year passed, so did the time separating her from the strain of bad relationships and bad Hollywood experiences. Some people were surprised when she didn't return to New York to live. After all, she had been her happiest there. People always loved her there; she was a legend. In Los Angeles, she was just another rich performer.

Of course, it wasn't as if the world had forgotten her. She still had loyal fans and she still was a guaranteed draw for live performances, but she didn't want to sacrifice her health for another national tour. She wasn't in the best of shape, and the last tour had almost killed her. Dying on the road was not her idea of heaven.

Many were surprised when she agreed to do a stint in Vegas during the last part of the year. After all, it had been a decade since she worked the Strip. And when she had, she hadn't really liked it. But now playing a show for laughs without moving from city to city appealed to her a great deal. And she would be in control, working a small, 300-seat lounge, with only a piano player. This wouldn't be a brash, outlandish spectacle—just a singer and her pianist. Besides, the kid who would be playing for her needed a break; his career had been down for a while, too. And Bette was looking forward to helping Barry Manilow out. The Golden Nugget, previously home to Frank Sinatra and Kenny Rogers, was looking forward to it as well.

It was ironic that the city that overdid every act it presented, and the woman who was normally as big an overdoer as any person could ever be, would come up with this new concept in big-name entertainment. Can you imagine what it would have been like to have heard Floyd Cramer playing for Sinatra in a 300-seat room? Can you imagine Diana Ross welcoming you to an out-of-the-way corner of the Strip and singing to just a few of the lucky people who loved her? Well, Bette and Barry were a pretty big story, too. This one-of-a-kind show would be announced, but it wouldn't come off. It took even bigger news to get Bette's name back in the Vegas press.

Bette had met a handsome German some two years before. His name was Martin von Haselberg, but most people knew him as Harry Kipper. He had no idea who the Divine Miss M was, and probably didn't care. She didn't really know who he was either. During their first meeting, they hadn't clicked. But two years later, when he called out of the blue and asked her to a concert, they did.

Von Haselberg was a commodities broker, but he also had a crazy stage act under his alter ego, Harry Kipper. He was three years Bette's junior, and in some ways shared a common background with her.

His parents were German, and he'd been born in Argentina, a land that was as strange to him as Hawaii must have seemed to Bette. He had spent a good part of his life alone, traveling and seeing the world, and he had always been quite successful in everything he had done. He had another personality—the zany Kipper—by which people often judged him; often, his true personality wasn't taken very seriously. Yet he was very well-read and extremely bright, and placed in a position to be able to understand Bette.

"It was just sort of instantaneous," Harry told a *Newsweek* interviewer. As unimpressed as he had been with Bette before, he was now head over heels. For Bette, the feeling was mutual. And for the next two months, as 1984 wound down, they were inseparable. Turning forty probably didn't hurt too much with Harry around to make Bette feel young again. The two of them always had a great deal of fun, and with this fun came a realization of just how much they complemented one another. Still, Bette's friends believed it to be just another fling.

Careerwise, everything she had recently planned had fallen through. Yet for the first time since she'd taken a sabbatical from entertaining over a decade before, Bette didn't care. So what if the radio stations thought of her as an oldie? So what if Hollywood didn't think she could work? So what if the tour bookers were becoming less-than-enthusiastic callers? She had her man, and she was just wild about Harry.

On a day in late December 1984, Harry asked her to marry him. She didn't hesitate. The woman who at thirty and thirty-five had pronounced that marriage was not a part of her future jumped headlong into this binding contract.

Over and over again she'd said she stayed away from marriage because she didn't want to battle through a divorce. And now she was willing to chance even that in order to give her hand a try at good old-fashioned love. It sounded so conventional—and it was—but it was also something that seemed to make Bette feel safer and more secure than anything she had ever before experienced. The world may have thought her to be on the downside of her fame, but she was on the upside of life.

The ceremony was one that every Bette Midler fan would have appreciated. It took place in a Las Vegas wedding chapel. She and Harry had driven there from Los Angeles and it was 2:00 A.M. one Sunday morning when they arrived. While much of the world slept, Las Vegas was still jumping.

Bette and Harry waited in line with dozens of other couples to get their license. Some were better-looking, others were not; some were old and some were young; some were even drunk; but none seemed happier than they did. From there they checked in at Caesar's Palace, a place befitting a Queen's honeymoon, changed clothes, and headed out to find a chapel.

Bette and Harry discovered the Candlelight Wedding Chapel sometime before 3 A.M., and after picking out a taped arrangement of Fellini's *Juliet of the Spirits,* the ceremony began. Harry was dressed in a nice suit, Bette in a grayish dress with strings of beads that swayed with her walk and the music. She carried a bouquet the chapel provided as a part of the service.

The man who married them was tall, dark, and looked slightly like Elvis Presley. When not performing ceremonies, he did impersonations of the King at parties. Who better to legitimize Bette Midler's—the "Queen of Trash"—relationship than a man who made his living based on another royal legend?

Both Bette and Harry cried a little during the ceremony, or so Bette claimed, and they both were supposedly very nervous. After accepting a single record (one of his own) from the Elvis-looking preacher, they returned to their suite and their marriage began.

Both of them should have been scared to death. Bette didn't really have a handle on much of Harry's background, and he didn't know that she had ever been to Hawaii, much less been raised there. It was hardly a situation that should have bred long-term happiness. Besides living with one another, they were going to have to actually get to know each other. Most couples who married had already done that.

Still, they had fallen in love with each other based on what they both were like now. Harry hadn't cared if Bette was good onstage—she could have been a lounge singer in Burbank and he would have still loved her. She was funny, warm, and gentle. This was what mattered. Nor did Bette have to know about Harry's London school experience, his history as an oddly dressed performer, or his family. She simply felt secure in his arms and well-loved.

Hollywood didn't see much of them over the next few months. As Bette told one reporter, "Why go out? The only reason you go out is to find someone to bring home." It was obvious by the moonstruck look in her eyes that she had her someone.

But she hadn't convinced too many other people that this was anything other than a lark. *People* magazine's annual poll voted her marriage the least likely to succeed. While this miffed Bette, it was really not important. She was happy, growing, and loving, and for her this was enough.

Meanwhile, just as it had been for almost two years, her career was floundering. While discussing the situation with Harry, he asked her what she really wanted to do. When she told him she wanted to make people laugh, he told her to try that. How? How about a comedy album? Soon she was parading through record stores making fun of every famous person in the world, or so it seemed.

About her husband, she said, "He's a German. Every night I dress up like Poland and he invades me." About the French she taunted, "The nation that gave us Renoir thinks Jerry Lewis is a genius." The album was a hit.

Mud Will Be Flung Tonight was an album that put Bette completely into the mainstream. And what *Mud* did was allow Bette an opportunity to harmlessly poke fun at the latest fads and stereotypes in society. In her own way, she was doing what Bob Hope's monologue had done for years, and was using her own style and wit.

The album was not as huge a hit as the soundtrack from *The Rose*, but Bette didn't care. It had been fun, and that was enough. Her interviews at the time gave her a chance to talk about what was really important to her—and that was Harry and her own self-respect.

"He put me back on the right path," she said over and over again. He made her happy. She didn't need to be a legend or always on top, because she now had everything she needed to make her happy. On and on she went, and it was all positive.

The last time that Bette had been so noncombative was when she'd been down and the world was a hell that contained no hope. Now she was up, and she wanted the world to know just how wonderful a place it could be.

This uplifting spirit had affected every segment of her life. Even the old house in the Hollywood Hills began to take on her charmed warmth. Her name might not have been in lights, but there was a glow about her. It seemed to be coming from her heart.

13

HAPPY AT LAST, BETTE SETTLED INTO A NORMAL LIFE, satisfied with her husband. She must have realized, however, that the best and biggest years of her career were behind her. After all, when she was hot she'd been young and very funky. Jane Fonda might get some wonderful roles at her age, as would a few others who could and would play mothers, but who would believe Bette as a mother? Or on *Dallas* or *Dynasty*? Probably only Bette and Harry.

Bette wanted to be funny and make people laugh, but no one was giving her a chance to do that on anything other than a stage or vinyl. She had the talent, but it was being wasted as the days passed. When interviewed, all she could do was talk about the kind of roles she would like to play, and dream of the parts that other actresses were landing.

Across town, another Hollywood legend was in

bad shape. Walt Disney Studios had not really had a hit since Walt had been running the business. The studio had tried to fit into the era, but their attempts had proven out of step with the times, and often downright embarrassing. *Tron* was an idea that should have worked—it had a well-known star, but people wanted to play video games, not take a trip through one. Everyone loves dinosaurs, so *Baby* should have made it big, too. It was extinct before it was even released. *Return to Oz* was a trip the studio shouldn't have booked. For Disney, the only glory at the theater seemed to be when their old classics were released.

Grabbing Michael Eisner, the studio gave it one more try by forming a new production company and attempting to make a film that could combine their old flair with a new harder edge. Their first film was directed by a former child actor, Ron Howard, and he made an unusual film about a man in love with a mermaid. *Splash* made a splash at the box office, and Touchstone Pictures was off and running.

Touchstone hired Paul Mazursky to work with them on their next release. They wanted something that would keep their momentum going, and soon discovered they'd chosen the perfect man for the project.

Mazursky, at fifty-four, had been in Hollywood since 1950, and had experience in every facet of filmmaking. He had acted in *Fear and Desire, The Blackboard Jungle, Deathwatch,* and *A Star Is Born.* He had written for both television and the movies, developing his talent on *The Danny Kaye Show* and later in his own films *Bob and Carol and Ted and Alice, Blume in Love, Harry and Tonto,* and *An Unmarried Woman.* All were legitimate hits. His movies showed a flair for taking risk, and this risk-taking was just what Disney was doing by coming out with films for adults.

Mazursky teamed with Leon Capetanos (they had worked together previously on scripts for *The Tempest* and *Moscow on the Hudson*) on a script that would poke fun at the establishment and make people laugh at themselves. Mazursky had seen a French film, *Saved From Drowning* by Jean Renoir, some thirty years before. In it, a vagabond who jumps into the Seine is saved by a bookseller who brings him into his home. Needless to say, the vagabond causes a great deal of trouble and creates many laughs.

Updating it, the two writers switched the film to the United States, and in many ways jabbed at their own lives and lifestyles. Rather than a vagabond of the French type, they came up with a street bum, someone who few people would ever acknowledge, much less invite into their homes. By placing the action in Beverly Hills, the contrast became both clear and funny.

Down and Out in Beverly Hills was a gamble for the new company. It poked fun at success, and it would carry an R rating (it was hardly a film in the image of Mickey Mouse). But if the script was a gamble, Mazursky's choices for the main parts went against even bigger odds.

Nick Nolte was the director's first choice for the part of the down-and-out bum. Nolte, whose career was at a low ebb, had once been one of Hollywood's hottest young actors. Now, his name was not going to guarantee a few million dollars in ticket sales. Nevertheless, Mazursky personally went to the actor's house, went over the script with him page by page, and sold him on playing the character of Jerry.

If Nolte wasn't hot, then Richard Dreyfuss was all but dead. He had exploded onto the scene in the mid-1970s, but as he had aged, his appeal had worn thin. There was little doubt he was a good actor—from time to time a great one—but he wasn't a tried-and-true comedian to make people buy tickets, and he certainly didn't have a corner on the sex-appeal market. Would he be worth the risk?

Finally, to complete his trio of stars, the director needed a woman who could be zany, smug, and uniquely off the wall. Not considering the warnings he'd heard about her temperament, Mazursky called Bette. She enthusiastically accepted the part of Barbara. This was the chance she'd prayed for, and one Bette knew she couldn't turn down.

As preproduction began, all of Hollywood was wondering if the folks at Disney, as well as the director of their latest project, had any idea what they were doing. All three of the leads had reputations of being hard-to-work-with egomaniacs. Various powers in the filmmaking establishment had written each of them off.

Added to his three sticks of dynamite, Mazursky had hired Little Richard as a costar. The aging rock star had been through so many different phases that few could keep up with what he was now embracing. At various times he had been gay, straight, a preacher, a singer, a semi-cross-dresser, a Christian, a Jew—and always he had been sold on the talents and charms of Little Richard. As if three huge egos weren't enough, here was a fourth to compete with them, and the guy wasn't even remotely considered an actor.

Jinxed should have worked. All the elements had been there to make it a sure hit. By the same token, *Down and Out* should have failed. There was no way that the director should have been able to keep this picture together, and then, even if he did, no one in the film was hot enough to draw movie patrons to see it. It seemed like a guaranteed way to throw away money. Still, the project went forward.

One of the smartest things Mazursky did was develop a relationship with each of his stars before shooting began. He explained to them what he wanted and how the film would be put together. He asked them to study and sacrifice, and he promised that he would treat them with respect if they did. And every one of them agreed to follow his plan and concept. Of course, particularly in Bette's case, if she wanted to work again, she had no choice but to be on her best behavior.

Marriage had been good to Bette in one way; it had given her a huge appetite for life. In another way it had been bad. It had also given her a huge appetite for food. She had gained twenty pounds since she and Harry were married. Barbara was supposed to be a sloppy sort of sleek, monied woman. And Bette could be that way, but the studio wanted her in better shape. She began to work with the famous exercise teacher, Jake Steinfeld, whose "Body by Jake" classes had made him a small fortune. After weeks with Bette, all he could claim was a lot of frustration and two pounds off her frame. Jake may have been distressed, but Bette was more concerned about the other facets of her character, and she was determined to learn more about the kind of woman she was playing. So, she did her on-the-job research.

She described her "research" to the press, and it sounded like a great deal of fun. "I walked all around Beverly Hills, and I shopped until I was blue. I decorated. I went to lunch at the Rodeo Collection and met all kinds of people. I met landscapers, pest-control people, and dry cleaners. You'd be amazed at how much the people who work the backstage of the rich and famous know about the people who are actually on the stage. I also spent some time with ladies who actually live the guru life. You know, rather wealthy women who are in search of fulfillment. Barbara Whitman is an amalgam of all those ladies. They're fabulous people in their own way. I mean, I wouldn't want to be in a world where they didn't exist."

The research changed Bette's opinion of her character and women who were like Barbara a great deal. Before getting a firsthand look, she had thought Barbara to have few redeeming values.

"I have no real empathy for matrons who don't have a lot to do with themselves," she said. "You know the type—so much time on their hands and no real imagination." But the director showed her that there was more to Barbara than just what she was seeing on the surface.

"Barbara is a soul in torment," Bette later explained. "The reason it's funny is that she really doesn't have anything to be in torment about. She has a lovely family, lots of money, and the freedom to do whatever she wants to do, and yet, she feels unfulfilled. She's a character who's searching blindly for the way to live her life. She's nothing if not an explorer of the psyche and trends. She loves a trend."

Bette had once been a trend-setter, and she had once felt very unfulfilled. She too had been searching for something while supposedly having everything. And Bette had felt great torment. The more she studied the part, the more she knew that she could play Barbara and be convincing.

"I was able to bring my own saltiness to the role. Barbara is quite cynical and more than a little angry. I have those elements in my own personality, but the rest was totally new to me. I've never worn clothes like this or nails like this. The whole visual thing is completely different from my own life. I can't tell you how bizarre it is to be playing a woman with grown kids!"

The filming—most of it done on backlot sets—went very smoothly. One of the things that had helped a great deal was Mazursky putting the actors through three weeks of rehearsals before loading the cameras. This time was probably responsible for defusing any potential personality clashes and ego bombs. Each of the actors received an opportunity to work with the other, learn to react to each other, and become comfortable with the crew. This stroke of genius changed the movie from a big-budget pressure cooker into more of a small, friendly production. For Bette it felt a great deal more like what she had done on Broadway than her other Hollywood experiences.

"We rehearsed for three weeks. If you're doing a stage production, that's not a lot, but it's a lot for pictures. It was a big help—a tremendous help. We knew each other, and we knew what the relationships were. We had explored all that, even to the point of knowing what our blocking would be."

Filming began in late May and was principally finished in twelve weeks. For the actors, the time was one of real joy. There were no hints of any frustrations with anyone or anything. The chemistry that should have led to an explosion didn't. Yet would it work at the box office? That question wouldn't be answered for six months.

While the joy of working again had caused Bette to relax and believe in the future of her career, another growing tragedy reminded her of her days as a struggling entertainer. The AIDS virus had hit the gay community full force, and many of her fans and former friends were dying. She had always felt a great compassion for this group of men, now placed even further out of the world's mainstream. With so many of them dying, and so many others scared, her heart ached even more than it had back at the Baths.

Bette couldn't find a cure for the disease, and it was not something to joke about. So she did the next best thing. She decided to raise some money to help find a cure. She held a benefit on her home ground, New York City, and Carnegie Hall was filled as Bette sang her heart out for the cause. Afterwards she told several reporters, "It breaks my heart . . . it's so sad."

There was an irony to Bette's emotion; the last time she had felt this sad was when she'd been feeling sorry for herself. Now she was happy and fulfilled, and she felt for the fans who she'd once mistakenly thought a part of her past. The hundreds of thousands of dollars she raised on that one night was much more than she'd ever made while playing for gay audiences at the Baths, but Bette was probably also aware that it was just a token compared to the jump-start this group had once given her career. After the show, she returned home, but she didn't forget the pain in the faces of some of her friends.

Even while the editing of *Down and Out* was still going on, word had leaked that Bette was not only good, but settled and easy to work with. While this was good news, she still was not exactly setting the world on fire. But there were offers and she jumped at the next good part that came down the tube, also with Touchstone. She and Disney seemed to be a part of the same family—their roots may have been different, but they were both originals. And they both seemed to need each other.

As Bette went to work on her next film, the year wound down. She was content, in demand on the interview circuit, and once again considered successful, if only mildly so in comparison to a few years before. All the bad memories of *Jinxed* were behind her. And Bette, now considered more of an actress than a singer, was able to sit back and enjoy the reviews of *Down and Out in Beverly Hills.*

Writing for *Insight,* David Brooks called the film "genuinely intelligent." He summed up a full-page review by concluding, "It is a comedy, and a very enjoyable one. At the same time, *Down and Out in Beverly Hills* is exceedingly intelligent, a movie that mixes the hilarious with the true."

USA Today's Mike Clark loved the film and raved about Little Richard's movie-stealing scenes. *Newsweek* proclaimed it "All in the Family, Bette Midler Style," seemingly implying that she had held it together.

In all honesty, Bette was not the star of the show, any more than the silly little dog who stole every scene was, but her character was one the world laughed at over and over again. She was a smash. And the film became a gigantic hit for Disney.

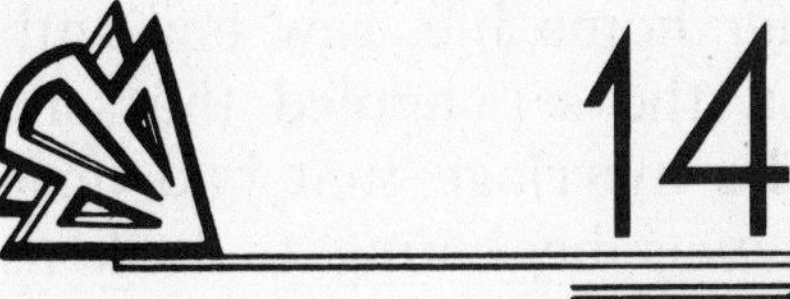

14

BETTE SCARCELY HAD TIME TO THINK OR RELAX BEfore beginning to work on her next role in the Touchstone film *Ruthless People.* Still, if and when she did have time to stop and read the "numbers," she must have been very excited. *Down and Out in Beverly Hills* was packing audiences in like there was no tomorrow. On top of this, Bette was winning both critical and fan raves for her part in the picture. Suddenly, the folks who had signed her to a three-picture deal at Disney looked very astute.

No one was more shocked over the acclaim and the more than $60 million in *Down and Out*'s ticket sales than Bette. "No one is more surprised than I am!" she kept telling interviewers. And perhaps in the most telling sign of how far her stock had recently risen, interviewers kept coming back to speak with the star again. At a time when Bette had a thriving marriage, a wonderful home, and everything she could want in her personal life, her career was riding high.

One of the most satisfying things she had accomplished was putting to rest all the prognosticators' views of her marriage. Everyone who talked with her, witnessed her home life, saw her with Harry in public or on the set, agreed that she looked very happy. The marriage that had once been expected to fail was beginning to look as solid as a rock.

Bette knew that she had to do *Ruthless People* from the instant she read the script. As she would tell the directors and later the press, "The screenplay was as funny as anything I've ever read." She was the first star hired for the film, and in many ways would be the anchor holding it together.

Down and Out had renewed Bette's confidence in herself and her abilities to sell tickets and get along with other creative people. It had also allowed her the opportunity to be funny on film—something she had wanted to do since her early days in New York. Just like Jack Carson, the great funny man of Warner Bros. fame during the studio's golden era of the 1940s, Bette had a rubber face. Her expressions could paint a thousand different scenes, and this element of her appearance made her perfect for comedy. Never was this seen more clearly than in *Ruthless People.*

People is probably the best-known of all Bette's films. It would be a huge box-office success, and it would lead to her signing a three-picture extension of her movie deal with Disney. And even though it really wasn't meant to be, this movie also became a Midler showcase.

As if sticking with something that would bring her luck, she once again played a woman named Barbara. This woman was fat, bossy, unhappy, and rich. Her husband, a part that short and diabolical Danny DeVito played to the hilt, had grown so tired of her that he decided to kill her. Before he could strike, a disgruntled former employee kidnapped Barbara, and the fun began.

What made the movie work so well was that DeVito's character didn't want Bette's character back. He didn't pay. The frustrated Bette, held in bored captivity in a basement for weeks, began to work out, losing tons of weight, and ultimately changing her disposition. For her, the forced captivity became a wonderful trip to the fat farm, and she even began to like her kidnappers. The one thing that kills her is that her husband will not buy her back. Probably the funniest line in the whole movie belongs to Barbara when she discovers that the ransom has come down from millions to $10,000 and it is still not being met. "Do I understand this correctly? I've been marked down? I've been kidnapped by K-Mart!" cried a disbelieving Barbara.

Bette may or may not have been the film's "bluelight special," but once again she loved the people with whom she was working, as well as her part. "I love the fact that she changes from horrible to wonderful in the course of the picture. I just loved the woman."

Two of the people Bette worked with very closely

were Bob Carriero and Jake Steinfeld. Over the little more than two months of filming, these physical trainers had to trim down the beefed-up Bette into a woman who looked good enough to have her own fitness video. For Bette, this meant sweating for her art. This kind of work is hard when one is twenty-five, but Bette was past forty, and her seriousness as well as her dedication to the physical regimen the film role required was obvious from day one. In fact, it was so good that many people wondered what kind of makeup or special film angles were used to pull it off. But when, just after the filming, a slim Bette appeared in public, everyone knew that camera angles had nothing to do with her new body.

While it is easy to say that *Ruthless People* succeeded because of the tremendous job that Bette did with the part of Barbara, it wouldn't do the rest of the company justice. From top to bottom, the film worked because of the excellent team assembled by Disney. Danny DeVito was super, and, like Bette, DeVito was beating the odds of being typecast because of his physical appearance. Judge Reinhold and Helen Slater were also good as the kidnappers, giving a sensitive and bubbling edge to their portrayals which Bette exploited for hilarious results.

And a great deal of the film's successful and necessary quick pacing could be traced to the directing team of Jim Abrahams, David Zucker, and Jerry Zucker. This triumvirate had first flown to fame in *Airplane,* but this was their first effort in a scripted comedy.

Others associated with the project included producer Michael Peyser and writer Dale Launer, but it was again the once-conservative Disney Studios's risk-taking that probably made the movie work. *Ruthless People* would outdo *Down and Out in Beverly Hills* and become the biggest Disney hit of the modern era. It was hilarious, a movie that even a dog couldn't steal. The critics raved.

Film Journal boldly stated, "Those who shook their heads at the thought of Bette Midler working for Walt Disney are now looking the other way as she racks up a pair of successful comedies under their banner . . . Midler steals the picture." *New York* magazine called Bette's performance "a clenched fist of fury . . . a comic fright." And yet, even with such glowing marks and her box-office appeal at an all-time high—she was in danger of becoming the biggest female draw of the late eighties—she didn't really have time to stop and notice. She was already working on another film.

If *Down and Out* and *Ruthless People* were wonderful opportunities for Bette, then *Outrageous Fortune* was heaven. In this, the last of the three films she owed Disney under her first contract, she would be costarring with Shelley Long, who had recently left superstardom on television for the unknown trials of moviedom. The two of them would hold the movie together. This meant being the real star, and being onscreen for almost the whole picture. It was a shot she had not really had since *The Rose,* and with two big hits behind her, she had the confidence and self-esteem to believe that she could pull it off.

By this time Bette was getting a host of offers and receiving more scripts than she knew what to do with. She was even hotter than she had been when everyone was telling her she couldn't miss back in 1982. No longer was she just another singer—a fad—she was thought of by the American public as a comedian, an *actress*. Bette was at a point where most actors and actresses only dream of being—working whenever she wanted, being offered more than she could do, and maintaining a happy marriage and normal home life far from the public eye. She was successful, but more importantly, she was settled.

Bette knew she wanted to do *Fortune* after reading the script for the first time. "I thought that it was the funniest script I had read since *Ruthless People*. I liked the adventure of it. I liked the chase."

She was given the role of a wide-eyed, cynical, directionless, overbearing, closing-in-on-middle-age, unsuccessful, and untrained Jewish actress named Sandy Brozinsky. Maybe Bette described this flamboyant character best when she said, "She is unflappable. She's been on her own a long time, she's independent, but mostly she doesn't take any guff from anyone which is, I think, one of her most admirable qualities."

In many ways, playing Sandy was not a stretch for Bette. She had been there, an outsider looking in, someone who didn't have the training or the culture to do certain things. She had people try to walk on her, and she had survived it all to come back and beat the odds again. Here was a woman who was tired of losing, and tired of being thought of as a loser. All she really wanted was a chance, and time was running out.

The interplay between Sandy and the sweet, demure, rich, cultured, seriously sophisticated character of Lauren, played by Shelley Long, made the film work. They weren't as much Laurel and Hardy as they were Hope and Crosby, two people teamed up out of a need to survive. They were rivals, and yet friends. At every corner they questioned the other, threatened to walk out, tried to outdo one another, and ended up with a fast and meaningful relationship that everyone who watched knew would explode back into rivalry as soon as they tackled their next adventure.

In a way, it was a modern *Road* film, as Sandy and Lauren got into constant trouble tracking down a double agent who they think is just another guy who loves them. The only thing they want is to find out which one of them is tops on his list. They didn't want adventure—they wanted to find love. What they got was an unending reel of trouble, involving the KGB, FBI, and CIA as well as black drug pushers, Indians on motorcycles, and suitcases full of money. What the audience got was a bellyful of laughs.

The unusual teaming of Long and Midler worked unbelievably well, and Bette enjoyed it very much. She admired the qualities Shelley brought to her work, and she loved her character of Lauren: "Sandy is a loudmouth know-it-all from the Lower East Side. Lauren is also a know-it-all, but from a completely different world. Their clash of values, as well as behavior, is what makes this picture very funny. Plus, there's a lot of warmth between Shelley and me that I think will come across on the screen."

Going on location to film the movie in New York as well as Arizona and Los Angeles meant that it was a lot harder work than Bette's first two movies for Touchstone. Still, with the crew she had around her, she issued no complaints. She was a delight to work with.

The director was Arthur Hiller, best-known for *Silver Streak.* He was "captured" by the relationship between the lead characters from the instant he began to read Leslie Dixon's screenplay. "I must say that I also liked the affirmation of the human spirit [shown in the film]. I hate films that are negative, even when they are dramas. I like to make films that are uplifting but also that reach the audience on an emotional level."

With his two leads, much more so than in Bette's two other hits, Hiller had a vehicle that made the audience care about their stars, not just laugh at them. While the story was unbelievable, it was one that contained enough of the trials of normal life that those watching could honestly relate to the lead characters. More than anything else, it was fun. With George Carlin and Peter Coyote offering support, the picture contained a million laughs.

For Bette, this should have been the happiest time of her life. She had earned her success, and she was on top. This new film had all the earmarks of being another huge hit. She had also just discovered that she was pregnant, and she was thrilled by the unexpected news.

Bette and Harry had not really planned on having children. It wasn't that they both didn't want them, but the odds against it were as large as Bette coming back after *Jinxed.* Bette had to take it a little easy on the set in order to keep the miracle she was now carrying. But she didn't mind slowing down a bit. If any pregnant woman ever had a glow, it was Bette.

But in the middle of the movie, and just after she discovered that she was expecting, her father began to experience serious heart trouble. Using every bit of her spare time, Bette would sneak away from the set or location and board a plane for Hawaii. Over the years, she and Fred had suffered through a multitude of differences, and yet they had, in a way, remained close. She would call him often, tell him of successes and failures. He would offer advice—advice both he and Bette knew would be ignored—but they would usually say goodbye on good terms.

Fred did like Harry, and the fact that his daughter had finally gotten married had pleased him greatly. Even as sick as he was, he'd been delighted when Bette told him she was going to make him a grandfather. It was obvious that he was very proud of Bette.

For weeks Bette challenged her father to hang on. She wanted desperately for him to see his grandchild, to know her child, so she pleaded with his stubborn nature to beat the odds and keep his tired old heart pumping. But he couldn't, and she had to take a break during filming in order to bury her father alongside her mother and older sister.

No doubt one of the things that helped her to recover was the rock of love her husband offered to her. Harry shared her pain, and rather than let her sink into a blue funk, he held her, comforted her, and then pushed her out again. But what even Harry couldn't understand fully was that not only had Fred Midler died before seeing Bette's baby, he had left her without *ever* seeing her perform—not even once. He had never been to a movie or a concert, and he regarded her work as vulgar—not something he would want to be seen watching or participating in. Fred Midler had had a daughter who had taken the world by storm, and all he had wanted was one who would stay home and give him grandchildren. But he died before Bette had a chance to become a real success in his judgment. In a way, he had cheated her one more time.

Nevertheless, Bette knew that her father loved her. And she knew that when he died, she had earned his respect in her private life. That was all that really mattered—her private life had brought her happiness and self-esteem, and her career and everything it offered was just the icing on the cake. Perhaps, in a way, Bette and her father had finally agreed on something after all.

15

IN NOVEMBER OF 1986, ON THE FOURTEENTH DAY OF the month—two weeks after the debut was supposed to occur, just a dozen or so years after she had played the Baths in New York City—a forty-two-year-old Bette Midler gave birth to a hefty little girl, weighing in at eight pounds and eleven ounces. In many ways, this spelled the ending of one life and the beginning of another. Being a mother, a serious one, meant that her image as the "Queen of Trash" was a thing of the past.

Bette and Harry named the child Sophie Frederica Alohilani von Haselberg. There is little doubt that the entertainer wanted to touch base with a great many facets of her life when choosing and using this unusual name. Sophie, no doubt, came from the entertainer who had so shaped her early career, the legendary Sophie Tucker. The Frederica, a name of German origin and history, could well have been a salute to her husband's roots, but it may have also been another way of remembering her father Fred—she had so wanted him to see her baby. The Alohilani was strictly Hawaiian, and this spelled a unique transition in Bette's thinking about paradise. Once she couldn't wait to leave it—now the memories were a bit more kind.

As a mother, Bette doted and glowed. She had beefed up to over 160 pounds during pregnancy, though, and she was going to have a long struggle in order to get back down to the form that had amazed movie patrons in *Ruthless People.* She vowed that she would slim down, but it was going to take a while. As she worked out, she must have been thrilled with the reviews that *Outrageous Fortune* was pulling her way.

"Shelley Long and Bette Midler together could energize even the most witless writing, but that's not an issue in *Outrageous Fortune.* Newcomer Leslie Dixon's script is witty and zippy, casting the twosome in roles they've virtually come to define; WASP princess and tawdry street trash . . . Midler and Long are outrageously funny." These words, penned by Mike Clark in *USA Today,* mirrored reviews everywhere.

Richard Corliss, reviewing the movie for *Time,* said, "Midler breezes through her role, looking fine and giving the punchlines pop." He loved the movie, coining a phrase that others would pick up when describing the relationship between the two leads: "The Lady and the Tramp."

New York magazine opened its review: "Shelley Long, who has perfect features and a perky manner, and Bette Midler, long of jaw and sounding like Telly Savalas, are awfully funny together." *Playgirl* played up the film, but saved its special spotlight for Bette: "Besides Mae West, there has never been a more adorable foul-mouthed babe onscreen than Bette Midler. In stretch pants, high heels, and full-on New York accent, Hurricane Bette would blow most other actresses out of the water."

Even with all of the singular praise Bette was receiving for her work in the picture, most reviewers and fans came back to the teamwork between Midler and Long. *People* probably said it best: "Bette Midler and Shelley Long bring out the bitchy, bawdy, best in each other in this breakneck farce."

Bette, meanwhile, was watching another bit of teamwork on the screen. She had taken a day or so off from the movies to shoot a video, "Beast of Burden," with Mick Jaggar. The two had clicked, and the video was very well-received. On top of this, Showtime was doing a special on the "Legendary Women of Rock," and Bette was one of the half-a-dozen they had chosen to interview and spotlight. Hitting with both the movie and the rock crowd, what else could Bette possibly want?

Disney came back with another three-picture deal, and to make it work, they allowed her to choose the production company and scripts. She chose All Girls Productions, a company that she had just put together, and signed the deal. Not only would she now make more movies, they would be all hers. A bit of a risk, but one she felt completely prepared to meet head on.

Evidently, so did America. In April, on ABC, she swept up the most awards on the American Comedy Awards. She won Best Actress in a Film for *Ruthless People,* Funniest Performance on a Record for *Mud Will Be Flung,* and two other awards—one for generally being funny, and the other for lifetime achievement (her work in concert, in film, on television, onstage, and on Broadway). A few days later, the American Cinematheque Awards presented her with an Outstanding Actress honor.

This award offered a unique opportunity for three giants of the music business to get back together again. Bette was joined at the dinner by Barry Manilow and Melissa Manchester. They had once starved together, and now the three talked about their early days. Surprisingly, many writers and music buffs, as well as most of the American public, were completely unaware of their mutual musical experiences in the early stages of Bette's career.

Manilow, who was supposed to have worked with Bette a few years before in Vegas, did manage to play a few songs, and urged Bette to get back together with him soon. He wanted to make more music. But Bette the mother and wife had little desire to stray too far from her California digs. She loved her new role, and she didn't want to leave Sophie for the road.

Manilow didn't give up. He wanted to renew his musical partner's interest in singing, and in late spring he called with an offer she couldn't refuse. He asked her to work with him on a June concert benefiting writer/director William Hennessey, a man who had given both of them big breaks early in their careers. Hennessey, once Bette's hairdresser in *Fiddler on the Roof,* had written many of Bette's early routines, and had been instrumental in much of what she and Barry had done at the Baths. He'd believed in them before either of them were close to being rich and famous. And now, Hennessey was suffering with colon cancer. He needed funds to pay his medical bills, and the kind of money he needed was the kind a teaming of Bette and Manilow could bring out. Bette couldn't refuse this old friend.

Bette and Barry did a few of the old songs, but even though their timing was not perfect, the magic was there. It was a night that the few who saw it would never forget. Most even overlooked the fact that Bette was still quite overweight. What mattered to them was she was there.

Somewhere, buried under a mound of good memories, the old news of Bette being hard to get along with had been lost. She was viewed as one of the nicest and most laidback people in Hollywood, and an ideal mother. Quite a change from the earlier public perception that wouldn't allow most critics and fans to take anything she did very seriously. No one had any doubt that Harry was due a great deal of the credit. But he simply pointed to his wife and said she did it all herself.

Bette was at a point where she did not have to work, but she wanted to meet new challenges as long as they didn't interfere with her home life. One of the first things that seemed to fit this formula was a book offer.

Little, Brown and Company approached her with

an idea of writing a book on motherhood. While they wanted something that wouldn't be irreverent, they did want something slanted in a different way than any other book written on the subject. They felt Bette was the right person for the job, and she wholeheartedly agreed.

Ironically, Bette's view of raising a child was different enough to be considered a spoof on its own in many people's minds. She wouldn't allow Sophie to watch television or listen to any kind of music other than what Bette thought socially redeeming. That music—a lot of Sinatra, Ray Charles, and a little Dolly Parton—was certainly good stuff, but it was just the beginning of constricting rules. These actually seemed to mirror a few that her own father had laid down early in her life. Fred Midler had wanted things his way in the forties and fifties, and his rules had been much different than the standards of the times. Now, Bette seemed to be just as out of step.

One positive way in which Bette was much different than her father was her expressive way of showing love. She was always cuddling and cooing, and Sophie's bright eyes would light up anytime her mother stepped into sight. The bond between them was very deep, and Bette seemed intent on keeping it that way.

For Bette, motherhood and success offered a host of magazine covers. Her face became splashed on newsstands everywhere. America wanted to know what she was wearing, what diet she was on, how she was raising her child, and what goals she had for Sophie. The ironies of this turnabout couldn't have been missed by anyone who had followed her roller-coaster ride in entertainment—from "Queen of the Gays" to "Mother of the Year" in just over a decade. From nervous breakdown to stable superstar in five years. Americans were quick to overlook and forget, and they often changed their minds. Bette had also come at least halfway to meet them. She had changed.

But she knew that she had a long way to go to cement this feeling, and couldn't rest on past successes. Even though Sophie was still young, it was time to get back to work. She wanted to branch out, and HBO offered her a way. A new special—not a musical, but a comedy—was hers if she wanted it. It could be totally her concept; all they wanted was for her to make people laugh. She agreed and signed. Here was something she could work on at home.

Along with the special, Bette had developed a new film, *Big Business,* starring another comedian, Lily Tomlin. Bette couldn't have been hotter, but Tomlin, like Midler, had suffered through some lean years after failing to catch the critical or the public fancy in serious roles. This All Girls Productions project offered her a chance to return to her roots by teaming with a can't-miss actress.

The story's concept was a funny one. Bette and Lily both played identical twins separated at birth. The twins are reunited by a fortune in money, and the swapping of places, trading of personalities, and laughs that result should help Tomlin reestablish herself in the film business. It would be ironic if Disney were responsible for resurrecting another antiestablishment entertainer's career.

After finishing *Big Business,* Bette began work on her HBO special. She had developed a concept of a trashy Italian show—an off-the-wall sendup of Johnny Carson. The host (Bette) and her guests would offer the worst in entertainment, while innocently believing they were the best. *The Beyond Mondo Beyondo Show*'s humor, satire, and performances, particularly of Harry Kipper, served to hit Middle America's funny bone like few of the cable company's comedy specials ever had. Bette offered Home Box Office a chance to gain back a little of the comedy ground that rival Showtime had claimed as its own. And *Beyond* offered Bette a chance to be creative in a way she hadn't been since Broadway, almost five years before. She could make fun of the people and institutions she loved, spotlight a few of her friends (this time her husband), earn a lot (though that was hardly as important), and write some of her own material. She could be zany, overplay her role, and take a few chances. In this case, it all worked.

As a matter of fact, whenever Bette reached out to take a risk, it always seemed to pan out. She had risked a great deal when leaving Hawaii for Los Angeles. A few months later, with few contacts and no job leads, she gambled almost everything she had on landing a career in New York. Then she did something that should have offered nothing but a dead end and maybe even have made her impossible to employ—and that was work in a gay club. But instead of failing, she was lionized.

When everyone else was into rock'n'roll, she was singing campy forties' tunes that shouldn't have worked with any audience, and she won a Grammy for it. And when a hard-edged rock film should have lost a bundle at the box office, she rode it out for a hit. Her concert tours, stage shows, and television specials were always a risk—always on the edge—but they worked. Everyone had told her that her marriage was a big risk, too, but nothing had ever made her as happy.

On occasion, when she had taken the sure thing, she almost always failed. Her beautiful mainstream music usually fell on deaf ears. Even *Jinxed,* the film with the so-called perfect costars and director, that should have been a big hit but was a bomb, wasn't supposed to be a risk. After all, she'd had total control.

Just about the only times she had not tasted success were when she'd taken a safe road to the top. Now, however, that she is as establishment as Kathleen Turner, and the hottest thing on film—will she continue to bet it all?

Perhaps, but the odds are against it. Bette has already said that she doesn't really want her daughter to know that much about Bette's early life until she is much older. Clearly she has settled comfortably into family life.

Bette Midler was raised an unhappy little girl in a supposed paradise. She left in search of rainbows on the stages of New York, Europe, Las Vegas, and scores of other cities, enjoying the high life and enjoying love before settling down in the surreal paradise known as Hollywood. Happy at last, Bette is returning to Hawaii. Having bought a chunk of the islands, she is building a home there for her family—attempting to prove that a person can go home again.

This Bette is not the same one who left Hawaii in 1963 (nor is Hawaii, a thriving state full of new people and opportunities, the same state it was then). Perhaps they have both grown enough to share their secrets of real beauty and serenity with each other. When Barbara Walters recently asked Bette to describe herself, she replied, "Tender, full of good will, enormously happy, and surrounded by wonderful people."

Nothing about Bette Midler has ever been predictable, not even her happiness. But it is love that has finally anchored her.

MOVIES

HAWAII (Bit part)
(1963)

A STORY TOO OFTEN TOLD (Small part, low-budget independent film)
(1972)

THE ROSE
(1979, 20th Century Fox)

Costars:	Alan Bates Frederic Forrest Harry Dean Stanton
Director:	Mark Rydell

DIVINE MADNESS
(1980, The Ladd Company)

Director:	Michael Ritchie

JINXED
(1982, MGM-UA)

Costars:	Ken Wahl Rip Torn Val Avery Jack Elam
Director:	Don Siegel

DOWN AND OUT IN BEVERLY HILLS
(1986, Touchstone)

Costars:	Nick Nolte
	Richard Dreyfuss
	Little Richard
Director:	Paul Mazursky

RUTHLESS PEOPLE
(1987, Touchstone)

Costars:	Danny DeVito
	Judge Reinhold
	Helen Slater
	Anita Morris
Directors:	Jim Abrahams
	David Zucker
	Jerry Zucker

OUTRAGEOUS FORTUNE
(1987, Touchstone)

Costars:	Shelley Long
	Peter Coyote
	George Carlin
Director:	Arthur Hiller

BIG BUSINESS
(1988, Touchstone)

Costars:	Lily Tomlin
	Michael Gross
Director:	Jim Abrahams

BROADWAY

Fiddler on the Roof
Clams on the Halfshell Revue (One-woman concert-style show)
Divine Madness (One-woman concert-style show)

ALBUMS

Atlantic
The Divine Miss M (1972)
Bette Midler (1973)
Songs of a New Depression (1976)
Life At Last (1977)
Broken Blossom (1977)
The Rose (soundtrack from the movie) (1979)
Thighs and Whispers (1979)
Divine Madness (1980)
No Frills (1983)
Mud Will Be Flung (comedy album) (1986)

Warner Brothers
In Harmony

SINGLES

Do You Want to Dance? (#17, 1973)
Boogie Woogie Bugle Boy (#8, 1973)
Friends (#40, 1973)

Married Men (#40, 1979)
When a Man Loves a Woman (#35, 1980)
The Rose (#3, 1980) (certified gold)
My Mother's Eyes (#39, 1981)

ABOUT THE AUTHOR

Ace Collins is a Texan with over a dozen books to his credit. A feature writer for three different national monthly magazines, he has written fiction, autobiography, and biography. His writings embrace everything from mystery to sports to entertainment. Over two million readers receive something he has written at least every month. Married, he has two children and spends his spare time reading, listening to music on his restored jukebox, and playing sports.